Debt No More

How to Get Totally
Out of Debt
Including Your Mortgage

Debt No More

How to Get Totally Out of Debt Including Your Mortgage

Carolyn J. White

Clifton House Publishing, LLC

ISBN 0-9661651-5-2
Library of Congress Catalog Card Number 97-77709

Introduction

TRYING TO DEAL WITH DIFFICULT FINANCIAL PROBLEMS can take its toll on many areas of our lives. Our marriage and personal relationships will be stressed, as well as our relationship with our children not to mention the hazards we place on our own personal health.

White has established a program to help you and your family to resolve this very difficult problem, and with your own personal commitment, you can be debt-free in about 5-10 years, including your home mortgage!

We have been taught to live in debt, to spend everything we make and then some. After all, most everyone else is doing the same thing, so it must be right.

WRONG!

Today, you will be given the knowledge and tools to free your life forever from all debt, if you will just heed the advice. **Only you can make the decision, so do it!** There is a whole new life out there just waiting for you to discover it. A life free from financial worries and cares. A life of financial freedom to do what you want, when you want, with all your needs and desires fulfilled.

Don't surrender to the old financial circumstances. **You can make your life what you want it to be!** Your financial prosperity is just a decision away!

From the Heart of the Author

RUPTURED DREAMS OF MY LIFE exploded across my mind as I witnessed the loss of everything I had worked for throughout my entire lifetime. I was catapulted into the deepest despair I had ever known. Everything was crashing down around me, and the feelings of drowning choked my very being. I welcomed thoughts of death as an escape. How wonderful it would be if I could just lay down and go to sleep, and never wake up to this horror in my life.

Finishing my "period of mourning," I just got plain mad! Mad enough to make a decision—"I am not going to take it anymore!" Having started with nothing in life, by working 12-16 hours a day, I had attained, at least on paper, millionaire status by the age of 35. By age 40, I was a multi-millionaire. At age 43, I had lost it all!

As I stood on the steps of the Courthouse, the auctioneer's last words resounded in my mind, "Sold for $5,000." My $2 million dollar house was just bought by the same bank foreclosing upon it for $5,000. My thoughts reverted to my meager beginnings and the circumstances that had brought me to this point of total darkness and humiliation. Many times we do not control these circumstances, no matter how well we plan. Having been a general contractor for twelve years, and being rather successful at it, it was the completion of three commercial projects that had brought about all these problems. Although payment was due on completion of each project, we were paid up to sixteen months late on these jobs. When the cash flow stops, you are only about 90 days away from total disaster—bankruptcy, and that is exactly what happened next.

Life is not always fair, but there is a happy ending to this story. I learned from my experiences. The biggest lesson I learned was that if I handled my finances like everyone else, I was going to be in the same position, or even worse than before. I learned that you must change the way you look at and handle your finances. I did, and what I have accomplished, you can too!

After losing everything to the bankers, and with my credit in total shambles, I had to start my life all over again. Financial survival for me and my family came only through my faith in God and my own ability. The chain of disastrous events had ended, and I was now at the bottom of the mountain looking up to the peak of the next, and wondering how I was ever going to get there.

With faith deep in my heart, I picked up the shattered pieces of my life and, as if trying to put a puzzle together again, I put the pieces back together. Those pieces that no longer fit, I threw away. I started re-building from a new foundation and found some clouds do have a silver lining, and you can too!

I cannot begin to tell you what a feeling of freedom that being debt-free can give you. It is like nothing else! If I can do this, you certainly can. I will share with you what I have learned and experienced. Hopefully, you will not have to experience the heart-ache and despair of failure as I did. I have put together for you the **DEBT NO MORE PROGRAM** from my experiences before bankruptcy, and from my survival afterwards, to lead you through the maze to the mastery of your own financial freedom.

I have a motto for my life that helped pull me through the hardships, and I would like to share it with you:

"IF IT'S GOING TO BE, IT'S UP TO ME!"

Acknowledgment

I HAVE NOT ATTEMPTED TO CITE in the text all the authorities and sources consulted in the preparation of this book. To do so would require more space than is available. The list would include departments of the federal government, libraries, institutions, periodicals and many individuals.

I sincerely thank all those fine people, who gave of their time to critique and review this edition. I know they are as proud of the part they have played and of their contribution to this work.

Copy editing by Alison Garrett
Book design and typography by Marc Bailey
Cover design by Robert Howard

How to Read This Book: The Focus and Progressive Order

- Review of the problems that plague and control us
- Why we must pay off our debts NOW
- Where does our money go
- Analyze the different types of debt, and what we can do about each of them
- Analyze present financial condition
- Create a time table to financial freedom
- Steps to putting the money back into your pocket
- How to stop unnecessary & impulsive spending
- Different ways we can save on everything we buy, and become a thrifty shopper
- Review of how to take back your life from your creditors

Notes:

(1) This is not an investment guide!

(2) The focus of this book is on getting you completely out-of-debt, including your mortgage, in the quickest time frame possible!

(3) Some items are reviewed in two or more areas of this book. It is not meant to be redundant! An item maybe reviewed first under the analysis of different types of debt, and then another aspect of the same item may be covered under steps to putting the money back into your pockets.

Contents

Warning—Disclaimer

Chapter 1

TAKE OFF THE ROSE COLORED GLASSES

WHAT WILL THIS PROGRAM DO FOR YOU?

THE DEBT NO MORE PROGRAM is the only debt elimination system you will ever need. It is the answer you have been waiting for. You can pay off ALL your debts and your home mortgage in 5-10 years!

How many times have you sat down to pay your bills only to find that there just was not enough money to pay them all? How many times have you said to yourself, "This spending has got to stop!" but just did not know how to go about stopping it? And finally, how many times have you told yourself that, no matter how hard I try, nothing seems to work for me! Each month that passes, I just get deeper and deeper in debt! How long have we watched the dreams of our youth fade away on the horizon of our lives, as we settle for meager existence? You can live the lifestyle of your choice rather than the one that circumstances forces upon you, and DEBT NO MORE is the answer!

MAKING THE DECISION:

Nothing is going to change in your situation until you make the decision to do something about it. Stop waiting for your ship to come in. Don't wait for The Prize Patrol to show up at your door. Sorry, but odds are against you!

Instead, emotionally ignite yourself! Get fired up! Create a burning desire within yourself to get out-of-debt!

If you are drowning in an ocean of debt, and the life preserver you have been holding onto has just sprung a leak, and there is no one around to save you, you are not alone! All of us have different incomes, and different levels of debt, but it is all relative! The more we make, the more we spend! It is a bad habit that must be broken if you are to conquer your finances. The mere fact that you are reading this book means you have taken the first step to pull yourself up by your boot straps and face the problem.

IF YOU DON'T KNOW WHAT IS WRONG, THEN YOU CANNOT FIX IT, CAN YOU?

Referring to Figure 1, the statistics show that only 9% of the population can retire with over $50,000 income. After working a entire lifetime, 91% cannot travel and do everything they want to do.

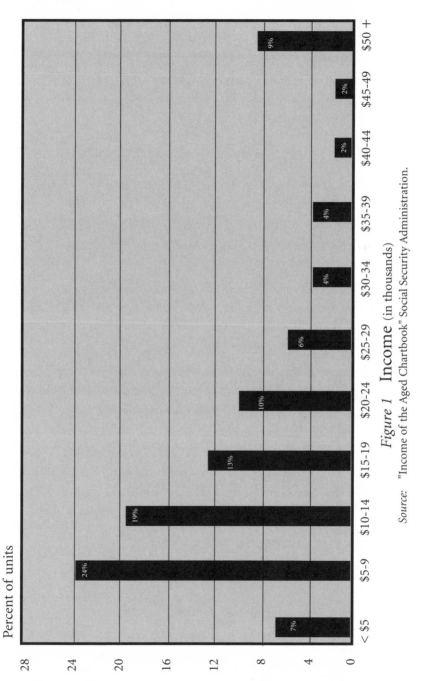

Figure 1 **Income** (in thousands)

Source: "Income of the Aged Chartbook" Social Security Administration.

Why are only 9% of the people successful? It is because they have given themselves goals to reach during their working years. They have made a plan, and they have worked that plan. You can create a plan right here and now that will free you and your family from the maze of alleys that have only dead ends. It is never too late.

WHAT ARE THE PROBLEMS WITH A LACK OF MONEY?

1. In your *Marriage*: Tension—Fights with your spouse.

2. In your *Lifestyle*: Trying to keep up with "The Jones", or siblings, or friends.

3. With your *Children*: Feeling hurt because you cannot give them what they want, or what other parents are giving their children, or simply feeling guilty for trying to give them everything.

4. In your *Employment*: Not being able to buy the proper clothing to make a favorable impression on your boss or your clients. Unable to pay for education necessary for promotion in your career.

WALKING A TIGHT ROPE WITH OUR FINANCES IS NO WAY TO LIVE. ONE OF THE BIGGEST REASONS FOR DIVORCE IN OUR COUNTRY TODAY IS LACK OF MONEY AND FIGHTS ABOUT MONEY.

LEARN FROM PAST MISTAKES!

- Mistakes you have made yourself.

- Mistakes made by your parents and relatives.

- Mistakes made by your friends and peers.

WHAT ARE SOME OF THOSE MISTAKES?

1. Not taking the time to learn how to handle money, or knowing where to go to learn. Most of us are never taught this.

2. Learning by example to live from paycheck to paycheck.

3. Having no discipline with money.

4. Living way above our means.

5. Being a shopaholic (Wearing a sign around our neck that says, "Born to Shop."

6. Trying to impress others by spending money we don't have.

7. Being impulse buyers, without thinking how we are going to pay.

8. Not having a plan.

9. Using credit cards instead of cash, and having to have it now!

IMMEDIATE FULFILLMENT OF OUR WANTS!

•   What problems are caused by our need to have everything now?

Most of us are living way above our means. The problem is that we are not willing to wait for something we want until we have the money to pay for it. Therefore, we go out and use that trusty credit card. We *can* have what we want, but with some planning and delayed gratification.

SOME OF THE FOLLOWING JUSTIFICATIONS MAY SOUND FAMILIAR:

1. We have been without for so long.
2. If I don't get it now, I probably will never get it.
3. It was my daughter's or son's birthday, and they have wanted it for so long.
4. I didn't have anything to wear.
5. It was our anniversary.
6. The old lawnmower was too much work.
7. I have just had it with the repairs to the old car.

What are these? They are excuses aren't they? I know we are all very familiar with every excuse in the book, because we have all used them to justify using that old credit card. It is so easy!

Chapter 2

PROSPERITY: THE ELUSIVE DREAM

IS PROSPERITY AN ELUSIVE DREAM FOR YOU? It is for a great majority of people. This is an awesome statement. I never believed it possible that in America, where in the past dreams became reality, that the tide would have turned against an individual fulfilling their dreams.

What do the statistics show? According to the Social Security Administration report, "Income Sources of Retired Persons", it is a bleak picture:

Number of Males	Yearly Median Income
91,254,000	$21,720
Number of Males 65 Years and Older	
12,829,000	$15,250
Number of Females	
95,147,000	$11,466
Number of Females 65 Years and Older	
17,847,000	$ 8,950

As if the median income figures are not bad enough, we are now going to take a look at the housing situation. Do you own your home free and clear? If you don't, this should be one of your major goals to the future. The U.S. Census Bureau report, Annual Housing Survey for the U.S., #H150/95/RV, Table #3-15, reflects the following:

- Of a total number of households in the U.S. of 97,693,000, only 24,518,000 own their homes free and clear (and of that number, 13,060,000 are aged 65 and older).

- We can see from these figures, roughly 25% of the total households own their homes free and clear, so that no one can take their homes away from them.

When bad times come, what will happen to the rest who fall in the 75% range?

How long can you survive when the cash-flow stops? As I learned from experience, the answer is, *"Not very long!"* I had worked hard all my life, 12-16 hours a day, 6-7 days a week, and I thought I knew what it took to achieve my dreams.

All this time, all that I had achieved (no matter what I was worth on paper) was a weight of debt that was a millstone around my neck. As soon as the bankers pulled the plug, everything fell down like a stack of dominoes.

As I pondered and tried many ways to return to what I thought was success, I finally awakened to the fact that no matter how hard I worked, it was not happening.

The government was making new rules and regulations, and the banks were making new requirements and restrictions. They were making it impossible for me to get ahead! Have you noticed how much more difficult it is now to make things happen than it was even ten years ago? It just seemed like I would row my little boat out into the middle of the river, and all of a sudden out of the clear blue, the rules of the game would be changed, and I would have to turn around and row my boat back to the old shore! And I thought, "How can this be?"

At this point, I started my own investigation. What I found out sent me into a state of depression! What it all boils down to is that only a few people in the world control the finances of the world, and that there is a plan to fleece your pocket book and mine, and keep you in the status of a "worker bee" for the benefit of those few.

Refer to SUGGESTED READING for a list of books that explains this in more detail, and I urge you to read those books and educate yourself. *Your first line of defense is knowledge, then action!* Don't take my word for it. Investigate it.

WHY IS IT IMPORTANT FOR US TO TAKE CHARGE OF OUR OWN FINANCES?

Why, because if you don't, no one else will! Nobody cares about you and your financial state of affairs except you! The government doesn't! The politicians don't! The bankers don't! You are only seen by them as a money source to keep them in office and pay for their wasteful spending. It does not make any difference what party they belong to! They will sing the song they know you want to hear, and as soon as the election is over, they march to the tune of their own drummer! Do not believe what these people tell you! If you think I am too critical, just look back over the last political campaign. Choose any politician and review their campaign promises. Then, look at their action and their excuses.

AVOID THE MEDIA HYPE!

Most of the major media (TV & newspapers) are owned by "The Establishment" or "One Worlders", as they are referred to. On national television, not too long ago, one of the major TV anchors admitted in an interview that most of their news stories come from the White House.

There is a newspaper that reports on the activities of The Establishment and has become a real thorn in their side, as they report the truth that you will not find in the major media and newspapers. See SUGGESTED READING.

WAKE UP AND SMELL THE COFFEE BEFORE THE CREAM SPOILS!

Profound insight into the future of our country and that of you and your family can be gained through educating yourself.

Bankruptcy filings are at an all time high in our nation. In 1996, 1,114,376 people filed for bankruptcy protection, which was a 29% increase over 1995. The first quarter of 1997 showed another record being set with 318,069 people filing personal bankruptcy. Believe me, it can happen to you!

We have to ask ourselves some questions and look at some definite realities that are happening around us right now. For instance, "Can you afford to be solely dependent on your employer for your income and livelihood?" I don't think so!

It seems like every day we hear about some major company laying off huge numbers of employees, many of whom have spent their lives working for that one company. I am referring to companies like IBM, General Motors, Mobil Oil, AT&T—and the list goes on and on. They are not laying off 10 or 15 employees, they are laying off 3,000, 10,000, 20,000, 30,000, and 40,000 employees, and most all of these people have families that are dependent upon their income. What are they going to do?

You can no longer think that your job is secure, because it is not! Too many factors determine the success or failure of a company, and too many people are waking up to the sad fact that they no longer have a job, and in far too many cases, their pensions are lost!

You are extremely vulnerable. If you lose your job and your income flow stops, how long do you think your savings will last, and how long can you survive? The majority of us live from paycheck to paycheck, and are only 90 days away from bankruptcy. The bills continue to come in, and the payments are still due! I know from experience that you don't last long!

Americans are among the smallest savers in the world. *Figure 2* gives some insight into the average American house-

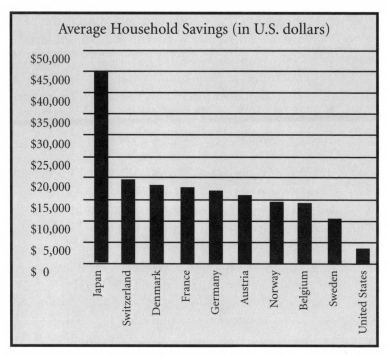

Figure 2
Source: "Where We Stand"

hold savings at $4,201 versus other countries of the world;
i.e., Japan at $45,118.

If financial problems are getting you down, where can you
get help?

The Fair Debt Collections Practices Act protects you
from abusive collectors. You can find help from a non-profit
service, which has about 1,000 offices nationwide. To find the
office closest to you, call the National Foundation for Consumer Credit at 1-800-388-2227. In some states, this is a free
service, and in others, there is a nominal charge. Consumer
Credit Counseling Service has helped many people dig their
way out of credit problems, and they can negotiate with

creditors to hopefully waive finance charges and late fees, reduce payments, etc. A listing of the Consumer Credit Counseling Service offices is listed for your convenience in the back of this book.

OUR ECONOMY WILL NEVER BE THE SAME AGAIN!

You must take the responsibility for yourself. You can no longer leave your future to the politicians and bankers or anyone else. Remember, if you believe just the *opposite* of what you see, read, and hear in the major media, you will have most of the true story. The American people are not as dumb and stupid as the politicians believe we are.

For instance: The government tells us through the media that inflation is almost non-existent. Now if you believe that, I have a bridge I would like to sell you.

All you need to do is go into a grocery store or gas station to see that this is not so. Compare the cost of a package of two chicken breasts in the grocery store over the past couple of years to today's prices. The gas pump reflects the same type of increase. Be aware of what is going on around you. Keep your eyes open!

Quicksand is waiting around many turns in the road— one of which is hyper-inflation. Unfortunately, in my opinion, our country is passing, or has already passed the point of no return. In just a very few years, the national debt will eat us alive. The printing presses for money have been running full tilt for some time now, and hyper-inflation will see to it that many of us do not survive the ordeal! You have to take your financial situation into your own hands to survive. You can survive by becoming debt-free.

Figure 3 shows the average household debt of Americans versus several other countries. Again, there is no big surprise

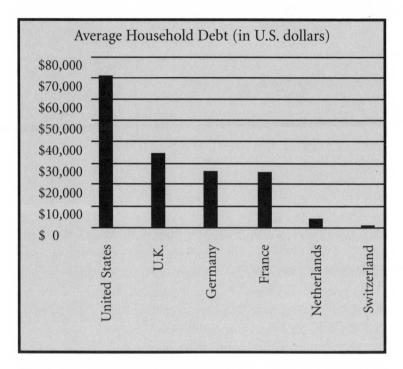

Figure 3
Source: "Where We Stand"

here! Not only is our nation addicted to debt, but our individuals and families are addicted. The average American
household owes $71,500.

Fundamentally, things are very wrong and the breaking
point is very near! No one can give you the exact day, or
month, or year that this will happen; therefore, you must
prepare on your own. You must become debt-free at the ear-
liest possible date. This is not something you sit around and
think about for a few more years. You have to do it now!

If you own your home, then no one can take it away
from you. If you own your automobile, then no one can take
it away from you. You must plan for your rendezvous with
financial freedom. It does not just happen by chance!

If you are totally debt free and owe no man anything, you can survive whatever happens. If you lose your job, you can live on very little without fear of losing everything you have worked for all of your life. Give yourself a worry-free future. Take control of your own destiny!

THE ESTABLISHMENT AND ITS RULE OVER YOUR MONEY:

There are two old sayings that I have learned to appreciate very much in my lifetime, and they are:

Those who fail to learn from the past are doomed to repeat it.
—Unknown

The more things change, the more they stay the same.
—Unknown

This is so true in the realm of government. Our politicians are selling us out. America has gone from being the biggest *lender* in the world to being the biggest *debtor* in the world! Does that tell you anything?

We are constantly manipulated by our politicians with the reporting of erroneous figures of our national debt, and changes in how it is figured; i.e., with interest rates, entitlements, etc. The increase in taxes that are not given much attention; such as, social security and medicare taxes on your pay, have been rising each year. The amount of money you can make to which the tax applies keeps going up. All this is done very quietly, and you tell me if you have seen anything in the media about this.

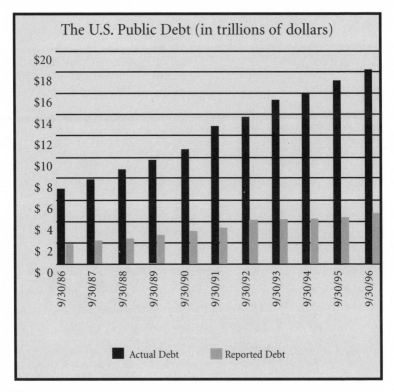

Figure 4

Figure 4 shows the national debt as reported by the government at about $5.4 trillion compared to the actual debt of about $18.1 trillion.

The economy is like a speeding freight train with no brakes! It has to derail around some unexpected turn. We are riding on the back of a tiger, and with most people there is no way to get off! You are being given the way to save yourself and your family and loved ones, and that is to become debt-free. It is easier than you may think!

Chapter 3

WHERE DOES THE MONEY GO?

HYPNOTIZED AND LULLED TO SLEEP. This describes the situation of most of the people in this country. This is a wake-up call for you and your loved ones!

I have gone through all of the aforementioned to hopefully bring you to this point. You must be motivated and hungry to get out of debt before you will do anything about it. And, if you have not yet assembled enough motivation to set yourself free from the vultures who are waiting to pounce on your lifeless body and worldly goods, then maybe what follows will inspire you to act!

THE RED CAPE AFFAIR:

- Who handles the money in your family? The following used to happen in my house all the time.

- My husband would come home and ask me the following:

"I make good money, and I bring it home to you, honey. What did you do with it?"

This is like waving a red cape in front of a raging bull! Now the fight really begins, and both persons go to bed angry!

You could be drawn and quartered with a statement like that, and most of the time, it is not warranted as we will see in the pages that follow. In fact, you have to be a magician to make all the ends meet.

The spouse who does *not* handle the burial of the paycheck does not truly realize what the problem is. This causes the disagreements and fights that produce a great number of divorces; i.e., fights over money and the lack of it.

The rescue ship has arrived to help you navigate through the rocky shoals to the safe harbor called financial freedom! Climb aboard and let's set sail!

HOW MUCH OF YOUR INCOME DO YOU PAY IN TAXES?

Well, let's see exactly where the money went!
See *Form A-1:*

*Please note there are extra forms in the back of this book for your use in calculating your own situation.

Do you know the rate for 1997 at which your federal income tax is figured? Below is a guide for your use.

FEDERAL TAX RATES
1997

IF YOU FILE	TAXABLE INCOME		RATE
	Over	But Not Over	
Single:	$0	$24,000	15.0%
	$24,000	$58,250	28.0%
	$58,250	$121,300	31.0%
	$121,300	$263,700	36.0%
	$263,700+		39.6%
Married	$0	$40,100	15.0%
Filing	$40,100	$96,900	28.0%
Jointly:	$96,900	$147,700	31.0%
	$147,700	$263,750	36.0%
	$263,750+		39.6%
Married	$0	$20,050	15.0%
Filing	$20,050	$48,450	28.0%
Separately:	$48,450	$73,850	31.0%
	$73,850	$131,875	36.0%
	$131,875+		39.6%

Source: U.S. Master Tax Guide

HOW MUCH OF YOUR INCOME
DOES THE TAX MAN REALLY TAKE?
Form A-1

	ONE YEAR	45 YEARS
INCOME:	$50,000	$2,250,000
LESS TAXES:		
Federal Income Tax (28.00%)	14,000	630,000
State Income Tax (5.75%)	2,875	129,375
Soc. Sec. & Medicare (7.65%)	3,825	172,125
State Sales Tax—multiply your gross income x 33% (1/3 is an estimate of your disposable income), and then multiply by the sales tax rate for your state: (4.5%)	743	33,435
Real Estate Tax—take from your tax bill	1,164	52,380
Personal Property Tax —from your tax bill	1,000	45,000
TOTAL TAXES	$23,607	$1,062,315
*Income after major taxes**	*$26,393*	*$1,187,685*

The total of all taxes divided by gross income equals your effective rate of tax: **47%**

(You are paying a whopping 47% to your various government bureaucrats!)

Note: We have not included self-employment tax, federal excise taxes on cigarettes, gasoline, etc.

LET'S TAKE A THOUGHT-PROVOKING WALK THROUGH FORM A-1

We are going to assume a $50,000 a year income with a working life of 45 years. Therefore, we have divided the income into two columns: *One Year* and *45 Years*. This will give you an idea of yearly and lifetime income and taxes for Married Filing Jointly.

We are assuming the following:

- 28.00% Income tax rate (Federal)

- 5.75% Income tax rate (State)

    (You may have higher, lower, or none)

- 7.65% Social Security & Medicare tax

    (6.20% Social Security on income up to $65,400 for 1997, and 1.45% medicare tax on *unlimited* income)

- 4.50% State sales tax

    (Yours maybe higher, lower, or none.)

Real estate tax assumes:

- $100,000 Home taxed at the rate of $1.164 per hundred of assessed value. Your town/city/county may or may not impose this tax.

Personal property tax assumes:

- Taxes on automobiles, boats, etc. between $800 & $1,200 per year. (You may not be taxed on these items, or your principality may impose some other form of taxation. Feel free to change the form to meet your needs.)

When you ask the question, "Where did the money go?", this is just the first part of the answer! We will explore the rest of the answer to this question in just a minute. Please take note that after major taxes, you only have *$26,393 left for the year*, or *$1,187,685 left for life* on which to live and enjoy life.

- As you can see from the percent of your income that you are paying in taxes, it is approximately 45-50%, at the 28% Federal Income Tax Level.

- You can also see from the previous calculations, that you will work until *mid-June* just to pay your tax bill. I bet that makes you happy! Also, keep in mind that we are not including ALL the TAXES that we pay, just most of them.

MORTGAGE INTEREST

- If you have a mortgage of $100,000 with a fixed interest rate of 10% for 30 years, you will pay a total of about $315,929 for that $100,000 house. (*Source:* The Complete Payment Book)

- In other words, you are paying $215,929 to the Bank in interest, simply for the *privilege* of using their $100,000.

LIFETIME PURCHASE/LEASE OF AUTOMOBILES

- During your lifetime, you are going to buy or lease approximately 20-30 vehicles.

- Assuming an average cost of $15,000 x 20 vehicles, this equals a total of $300,000, not including the interest on the loans!

WHAT IS THE BOTTOM LINE?:
(Taken from Form A-1)

	<u>45 YEARS</u>
Total Income	$ 2,250,000
Less Total Taxes Paid	- 1,187,685
Less Mortgage & Interest	- 315,929
Less Automobiles Purchased/Leased	- 300,000
(Interest on Auto Loans is not included)	

Bottom line—This is all that is left
for you and your family for
the rest of your lives!   <u>*$ 416,386*</u>

Is this an eye-opening experience or what? After working for 45 years, you only have $416,386 left. Let's do an analysis on what other expenses must be deducted from your remaining $416,386:

- Interest on the 20-30 automobile loans.

- Medical & dental insurance (Assuming you must pay your own or the co-pay portion.)

- Automobile insurance

- Homeowners/rental insurance

- Life insurance

- Food and clothing

- Utilities

- Furniture and furnishings for your home

- Gifts: birthdays, anniversaries, holidays, etc.

- Vacations and entertainment

- Emergency expenses (new furnace, hot water heater, etc.)
- School & College Expenses
- Investment for Retirement
- Repair & Maintenance of Home & Autos
- Gasoline for Autos
- Veterinary Expenses for Pets
- Child Care
- Alimony and Child Support, if applicable
- Miscellaneous everyday Expenses

With only $416,386 to cover a lifetime of the above expenses, is there any wonder why we are having such a hard time making ends meet? Or what is more, having anything left over to enjoy?

Up to this point, we have been looking at all the *bad news.* Let's turn the page now and take a look at the *good news!* There is a way to beat the system and stop groveling in the pits of despair, and that is to be debt free.

We are now going to take a look at *specific problems* we all encounter, and the *specific solutions* to those financial problems!

GOOD NEWS COMING UP!

Chapter 4

IT'S TIME TO BREAK THE CHAINS OF DEBT

CREDIT CARDS

CREDIT CARDS ARE THE MOST INGENIOUS SCAM being perpetrated by banks on the unsuspecting public! You may be paying as much as 25-32% interest and don't even know it!

Of all the different types of debt that we incur, credit card debt is by far the worse. Banks are very clever about putting things they don't want you to know in print so small you need a magnifying glass to read.

There are two types of credit cards, secured and unsecured. Most people have an unsecured, or regular VISA or MasterCard. However, if you have had credit problems, probably the only card you can get is a Secured card.

Note: If you have never established credit before, a Secured card is an excellent way to do it.

Secured Visa or MasterCards look
exactly like a regular credit card. It does not show on the face of the card that it is a Secured card, so no one except you and the bank know the difference.

Note: If you have had a bankruptcy that is still showing on your credit report, I would suggest calling the banks first before you apply to see if it makes a difference. You definitely do not want to show too many applications for credit on your credit report. I will advise later in this book where to find the best credit card companies.

A Secured credit card, as its name implies, is secured with collateral—*your money*. In other words, you put up the money in a savings account held by the bank, which may or may not pay interest to you; however, you cannot touch this money.

The amount of the collateral can be pretty much what you want; i.e., $500, $1,000, or more. Some banks will allow you to use 100% of the deposit as your credit limit, and some will only allow 50% as the credit limit. A Secured card normally carries a higher interest rate. After my own bankruptcy, this was the only way that I could start to re-establish my credit, and it definitely pays to check out several banks before deciding on one!

Regular Visa and MasterCards can be
obtained by anyone with good credit, and they do not carry the extra requirements of the Secured cards. Again, definitely check out several banks before you decide, and after going

through the exercise with *Form B-1*, you may want to change to another bank. I would also suggest that if you use a card for business, that you keep it separate from your personal charges. In other words, use one card for business only, and another card for personal use only. Do not mix the two!

You may wish to turn back and forth in the book now as we go into detail on *Form B-1* (CREDIT CARD ANALYSIS). Please turn now to *Form B-1*, to review same and then return here as we start our credit card analysis:

GRACE PERIOD:

Beware of a card that has no grace period. You definitely do not want this card! Why? Because your interest starts from the very day you charge your purchase.

A grace period of *25 days* is preferred! I might add that you can get almost 48 days grace if you look at your statement for the closing day of the cycle, and say it is the 18th, wait until the 20th and then charge. You are then billed on the 18th of the next month and you have your grace period to pay, thus giving you almost 48 days without interest if paid in full.

BILLING CYCLES:

Do not accept a 24-day cycle. A 24-day cycle will give you 14 bills a year instead of 12, and since you do not have 14 months in a year, you can see that this could cause a big problem.

A *30-Day* cycle is best! Make sure you know the day of the month that the billing cycle starts. Find this on your statement.

ANNUAL FEES:

The ideal card has no annual fee, but in taking into consideration all the other factors with the card, you may decide on a card with a fee. However, make sure it is as low as possible. Also note after you have had the card awhile, and another card offer comes in with no fee, you can call the bank and negotiate for no fee as well as a lower interest rate. Many banks will do this just to keep from losing your business.

BALANCE TRANSFER FROM OTHER CARDS:

1. Be very sure you know when the interest will start on a balance transfer. Some banks will treat the transfer as a cash advance, which means the interest can start on the day of transfer and the interest rate can be higher.

2. The interest rate on a cash advance is normally higher than on a regular charge.

3. Some banks will assess a surcharge for this service. If so, what is it?

CASH ADVANCES:

1. What is the interest rate on a cash advance? You can be sure that it is very, very high! I would rather see you charge a purchase than to take a cash advance. On a regular purchase you are going to pay a lower rate, but on a cash advance, they are going to sock it to you with double digit rates.

2. When does the interest start on a cash advance? Again, make sure you know if the interest starts immediately or whether you get the 25-day grace period.

INTEREST RATES:

1. Special offerings with extra low interest rates of, say, 5.9% or 7.9% are designed to sign up new card holders.

These rates are short lived and usually revert to a variable rate, which is much, much higher.

2. Department Store credit cards usually carry higher rates of interest. Their come-on is to give you 10% off on your purchases the day you apply for their card. Normally, this discount applies *only* to that day's purchases.

HOW ARE INTEREST RATES FIGURED?

There are many different ways the banks can figure the interest rates. You have to thoroughly examine the back of your statement which shows the different methods. On the front of your statement, it will show which method they are using. Some of the more common methods are:

AVERAGE DAILY BALANCE METHOD:

This method takes the daily balances for the cycle and divides by the number of days in the cycle to come up with your average daily balance.

PREVIOUS BALANCE METHOD:

This method simply takes the balance owed at the end of the previous month, and your interest is charged on that balance no matter what you have paid since then. Many free cards use this method.

TWO-CYCLE BILLING:

With this method, you have to pay off the entire card balance for two consecutive months; i.e., you paid off your balance in June but did *not* pay off your balance in July, then you would be charged interest for both months. You lose your grace period!

LATE PAYMENT AND MISCELLANEOUS FEES:

1. If your payment is received late, what is the charge? Is it $10 or $20 or what?

2. Some banks, in an attempt to get every penny they can get, consider you a "Free Loader" if you do not use your card, and set penalties for not contributing to their pocketbook! The common fee for this is $25.

Before we leave the subject of credit cards analysis, I would like to discuss credit card insurance offers:

Many cards take pride in offering you credit card loss and theft protection insurance for *an additional fee*. Some of the premium cards (Gold, Platinum, etc.) include this free as an extra to sell their cards.

1. You do not want this insurance, and you certainly do not want to pay extra for it.

2. By law, you are liable for only $50 if your card is lost or stolen, and you report it within two business days! So why pay extra for it?

CREDIT CARD ANALYSIS Form B-1				
Credit Card Name or Number:				
Grace Period: None 25 days Other				
Billing Cycle: 24 days 30 days What day of the month does the cycle start				
Annual Fee: None How Much				
Balance Transfer from Other Credit Cards: When does the interest start accruing? Day of Transfer Next Cycle Is there a surcharge for the transfer - how much Is the transfer treated as a Cash Advance - What is the interest rate				
Cash Advances: What is the interest rate Does the interest rate start immediately				
Interest Rate: Is it a special offering rate and for how long - What is that rate Fixed Rate - What is it Variable rate				
Late Payment Fee: How much				

NOTE: Refer to your monthly statements or initial offering information to fill out this form.

IS IT REALLY WORTH THE COST?

Now that you have completed the Credit Card Analysis, we are going to look at your savings if you switch to a card with a lower interest rate. Let's cut down the interest cost until we have them paid in full!

CREDIT CARD INTEREST COST ON AN ANNUAL BASIS

Average Balance	15%	17%	18%	19%	20%
$ 2000	300	340	360	380	400
$ 3000	450	510	540	570	600
$ 5000	750	850	900	950	1000
$ 7000	1050	1190	1260	1330	1400
$ 9000	1350	1530	1620	1710	1800

Note: If you are paying 20% interest on $9,000 average yearly balance, it is costing you $1,800 in interest a year. By switching to a card charging 10%, you will pay $900, thus saving $900 a year.

THERE! YOU JUST GAVE YOURSELF A RAISE!

WHERE CAN YOU FIND THE BEST CREDIT CARDS?

You can obtain a list of banks offering the lower rates and no annual fee by calling or writing:

Send $4.00 to:

> BANKCARD HOLDERS OF AMERICA
> 524 Branch Drive
> Salem, Virginia 24153
> Phone: (540) 389-5445

Send $4.00 for a *Secured* Credit Card List.

Note: Bankcard Holders of America offers a one-year membership for $24.00 which gives you all of the above plus a few extras.

You can order a list for *regular* credit cards and *rebate* credit cards from:

> RAM RESEARCH—CardTrak
> P. O. Box 1700
> Frederick, Md. 21702
> Phone: (301) 695-4660

Send $5.00 for a REGULAR card list
Send $12.00 for a REBATE card list

DEBIT CARDS:

Debit cards are *not* credit cards.

They look just like your VISA or MASTERCARD, but when you use them, the amount is deducted directly from your checking account, mutual fund, etc.

Debit cards offer you better management of your expenses, because generally if you do not have the money in the account, you cannot use the card.

Form B-2 (CREDIT CARD EMERGENCY CONTACT LIST) follows. Please take a moment to fill it out and put it in a safe place in case you lose your cards or they are stolen. This will give you a ready reference so that you can give immediate notification to the credit cards companies to insure that your only liability in the loss of these cards is $50.00. Remember, notification must be given within two days to limit your liability!

CREDIT CARDS EMERGENCY CONTACT LIST
Form B-2

Card Name & Address	Phone # to Report Loss	Account Number	Who Carries This Card*
_____	_____	_____	_____
_____			
_____			
_____			
_____	_____	_____	_____
_____			
_____			
_____			
_____	_____	_____	_____
_____			
_____			
_____			
_____	_____	_____	_____
_____			
_____			
_____			

H=Husband, W=Wife, B=Both, O=Other _____

CUT THE COST OF CREDIT CARDS UNTIL THEY ARE PAID IN FULL!

A little further in this book entitled, "What is your present financial condition?", we will cover steps that will give us victory over all our finances. But for now, we are going to take some interim steps to start bringing down the costs with credit cards until they are paid in full. Having just gone through the exercise of credit card analysis and savings by switching to a lower interest rate card, we should all be ready for the next step.

Credit Card Junkie—Born to Shop! If this description describes you or your spouse, it is suggested that you turn to the section on SUGGESTED READING. There are some excellent books listed that will help you to determine what category of spenders you fall into, and will help you to overcome this addiction. I know it is an addiction because at one time I was in that category. I could have worn a sign around my neck, "Born to Shop." It was spend, spend, & spend some more, with absolutely no thought of how I was going to pay for it! I guess I assumed there was a money tree growing in the back yard, and all I had to do is go out and pick the dollar bills off the tree! Or, just maybe, rub the magic bottle three times, and the genie appears to grant my every wish.

We have to change our mental way of thinking about credit cards and what motivates us to use them. Many times our spending habits are a direct result of what we learned in our childhood, and by the examples given us by our parents. Too many of us had parents who had desperate financial situations, and we learned by observation to think that this was the only way to conduct our own finances. Thus, we have never sat down to figure out where the obsession comes from that we have to keep buying and buying and buying. Please read some of the recommended books on this subject, as it will give you understanding and willpower to help you to build a worry-free future for you and your loved ones.

Stop sabotaging yourself with these bad habits. Experts have found that a habit, good or bad, can be changed in 21 days of consistent action. That is all it takes!

Speaking of parents, I would like to tell you a true story in my life. I was fourteen years old and school had just let out for the summer. Having always been an entrepreneurial person for as long as I can remember, I decided to make money this particular summer by starting my own doll manufacturing business.

I would take the bus into town to buy all the necessary items and then make my doll samples in various colors. The samples were then placed on display with various beauty salons and gift shops. It was not long before the orders started rolling in. The dolls were sold for $2.75 each. Well, by the end of the summer, I had profits in my vanity table drawer of $600.00! From that time on, I completely paid for my own clothing, lessons, and school needs, so that my parents only paid for shelter and food.

My father had struggled all his life, and mother never worked outside the home, so there was not very much money left to spend on my wants, like modeling school and voice lessons.

After the summer was over, Dad decided I was doing better than he was, and so he asked if I wanted to handle the family finances (at age 14), and I agreed to do it. Dad would bring his pay home in cash, and I would put the money into individual envelopes for the respective expense. I would give Mother the money for the grocery store, and Dad the money for gasoline, etc.

Well, it was not long before there was a new Cadillac car sitting in the driveway, *all paid for!*

To summarize this connection with parents, even though Dad and Mom really didn't have a lot, they did show by example many positive traits. For instance, Dad only brought home about $3,000 a year in those days, which was just not enough to pay all the expenses of the family. So, he bought a small piece of land, and ALL of us embarked upon the process of building the house. This was very hard for a young girl who wanted to be a model., to have to tear her hands up mixing concrete, laying brick, hammering and nailing, and gathering stones by hand to go around the foundation! However, many constructive lessons were learned along the way! All of which were to my benefit in the years that followed.

The house construction was done on a PAY AS YOU GO commitment, so when it was finished, it was paid in full. What a feeling to have your home paid off.

It does not take very much money to live if you are not paying out the majority of your income for housing!

Parental examples are very important! If you were fortunate enough to have received good examples in your growing years, more power to you. But, if you were not so blessed, it just means you have to work harder to overcome the negative, and to absorb the positive ones as illustrated in the books recommended for your reading.

Now, back to credit card debt—*How does this happen?* Just a little at a time! Here is a little exercise to go through. After you have read, close your eyes and just mentally go through the following in your mind:

> *When we are out charging everything in sight, it is like pushing a one-pound snow ball off the top of a mountain, and by the time it reaches the bottom, it now weighs about 500 pounds.*

Reality hits only when we have to start paying off that 500 pound snowball, and realize we do not have the money to pay, so we start paying only the minimum payment due as shown on the monthly statement.

Now picture in your mind that 500 pound ball of debt and try to push it back up to the top of the mountain. Really put your back into it! Feel the struggle.

I had an old boss whose favorite saying was, "If you are going to dance, you are going to have to pay the fiddler!" No truer words were ever spoken, as he was speaking from his own experiences in life as well.

HOW CAN WE CHOP THAT 500 POUND BOULDER OF DEBT DOWN TO SIZE?

1. Get rid of the credit cards! Take them out of your wallet and lock them up. It is hard to charge if you do not have the card in your pocket. It forces you to plan and think before you can use it, if it is out of your reach!

    After completing *Form B-1*, Credit Card Analysis, you should now have a good idea of which card you should keep (under lock & key, of course). If none of your cards measure up, you may want to apply for another card and transfer balances to the new card at a lower interest rate. We will discuss other avenues of debt consolidation later.

2. In Item #1 above, I really wanted to say cut up those credit cards and send them back to the banks with a letter telling them to cancel the cards, but, I think most people probably would have had a heart attack at the very suggestion!

Our goal to the future will be to keep only one card to use for hotel reservations, purchase by mail, identification, etc. The general rule of thumb will be: never charge more than you can pay off totally when the bill comes in.

3. Stop going to the shopping mall, or any other place where you are tempted to spend money! This is no longer a place of recreation. Believe me, my spouse and I used to go to the malls because we did not have money to do anything else, and guess what happens when you go looking in the windows. You are surely going to get in trouble! There is always something in the store that just seems to call your name.

4. Stop reading the Sunday newspaper sale ads! What a challenge it was for me to conquer this addiction. I would rationalize to myself what a great deal this was, and I didn't want to get left standing on the dock. What I failed to realize then was that many of the prices are marked up, so they can mark them down, so you think you are getting a real deal.

For me, however, it didn't make any difference. I was addicted to any sign or advertisement that read: Sale—Sale 20%, 30% up to 50% off. Now I know that this kind of advertising does *not* influence you to buy. Does it?

WHY IS CREDIT CARD DEBT SO COSTLY?

RULE OF THUMB:

For every $10 you charge, and then pay the minimum payment as shown on your statement, it will cost you about $40 to $50.

For example:

Our favorite store is having a 50% off sale and we have just found $ 6,000 worth of the most useful and/or beautiful whatever (could be clothing, furniture, lawn mowers, tools, etc.), and the best part is, we are going to save ourselves $3,000!

We don't even hesitate, and using as many rationalizations to ourselves as we can dream up, we pull out that trusty credit card and say to the salesperson, "I'll take it!"

What did we just do? Basically, our only concern was hoping that we had not exceeded our credit limit! I am sure you have experienced this situation, as I have. Handing the credit card to the salesperson and holding your breath and praying that the lights and bells will not go off indicating that your credit card has been turned down because you are over your limit. You may say to yourself, "Wow, that was close," as the salesperson hands you back your card and asks you to please sign here.

Since we did not have the cash to pay for our purchase, *here is the result*:

1. We charged $3,000.

2. We pay only the minimum payment shown on our Statement with an interest rate of 17.9%.

3. It will now take us about 32 years and 2 months to pay off this debt, and you will have paid $17,000 in interest. Add to this the original amount charged of $3,000, and you have paid out $20,000 for that $3,000 item. Remember, this $20,000 is after tax money. Just think how much you have to earn before taxes to pay off the $20,000.

Note: Have you ever noticed when you are making the minimum payment that the next months statement will have a lower minimum payment due. You see, the banks don't want you to pay them off. They want to keep you working for them as long as they possibly can!

CREDIT CARD REVIEW—LET'S HIGHLIGHT A FEW ITEMS:

1. Credit Unions are normally the best place to get a credit card, as their profits go back to their members.

2. Frequent Flyer Cards—You are going to have to charge up to about $25,000 to get a free round trip ticket. Most cards give back .25% to as much as 1.5%. Multiply that one out.

3. We looked at many tricks that the banks play to get your business; i.e., misleading ads/offerings, disappearing or no grace periods, different methods of calculation of interest, etc.

   Now that you have done the credit card analysis of your current cards and/or those being offered to you, decide on the best card. If the best card is the one you presently have, Good! If your present card would be fine with just a reduction in interest or elimination of annual fee, then call the bank and ask for what you want. If you have an offer from another company, they will very often come down on their rates. It is worth a call.

   If the best card is one being offered to you, then transfer the balances from the higher rate interest cards to the new one. First, find out the closing date and make your transfer about two days later. This will assure the greatest number of days before your next payment is due.

4. By switching to a much lower interest rate card, you will save money, even while you are making payments. If

you're presently paying 18% and you switch to a card with 9%, you have saved 50% of the interest you would have had to pay.

For instance, if you were paying $1,000 a year in interest, you would now only pay $500 a year in interest. You can now put that extra $500 towards paying off the card!

AUTOMOBILES—PURCHASE OR LEASE:

You must first determine whether you want to purchase or lease. I prefer purchase, as leasing can cost up to 15% more. Leasing is best reserved for businesses.

If you have a PC computer with Windows 95 or Windows 3.1, you may want to consider a software program called *EXPERT LEASE PRO*, which will give you the pros and cons of leasing. It will also show you how to save money, and will educate you to the point where you cannot be taken advantage of, because you will now know the car dealers little secrets! See SUGGESTED READING for details.

- During the elimination of your debt, it is not suggested that you buy a new car or lease a car. Instead, if you must replace your present car, purchase a used car at least one to two years old, with low mileage. Remember your goal!

PURCHASE YOUR NEXT AUTOMOBILE:

After you have made the determination of which vehicle you want, there are several steps you can follow:

1. Go to the dealership, write down the base price of the vehicle you want, and a listing of all equipment you want on the car and their individual prices.

2. Now you are ready to do a little investigation to make sure you do not end up being taken on an expensive ride by the dealer.

   You can order a report on the vehicle you want from *Consumer Reports* (Telephone: 1-800-594-9245) at a cost of $12.00 for the first report and $10.00 thereafter. This report will give you a complete list of costs. It shows the dealer invoice price, and the sticker price with all options. *Consumer Reports* also gives a depreciation rating, which predicts how well the vehicle will hold its value. They give equipment recommendations, and advice on negotiating a fair price.

3. Consider selling your old vehicle yourself instead of trading it in on the new one. The dealer will only give you wholesale value for your car. If your car is in too bad a shape to sell yourself, then trade it in. Advice on selling your car yourself follows.

Armed with the information in the *Consumer Reports* on your vehicle, you are ready to do battle with the dealer. This can be done in three ways:

FACE-TO-FACE NEGOTIATIONS:

This is hard for many people to do, but if you are not intimidated easily, this may be the way for you. See *Consumer Reports'* advice on accomplishing this feat.

WRITE A LETTER TO SEVERAL DEALERS:

Simply state that you are going to purchase this vehicle immediately.

Give a complete list of options and accessories, and advise if they quote on other items, they are to be listed separately, and to include all final costs, such as taxes, tags, etc.

Tell them you are getting quotes from several dealers and you are asking for their most competitive quote.

OR, JOIN A CLUB BUYING SERVICE:

Such as:

> THE CONSUMER CAR CLUB
> 350 California Street
> San Francisco, Ca. 94104
> (800) CAR-CLUB

They can even help you factory order a vehicle, if you are not in a hurry, and can save you even more money.

FINANCING YOUR NEW VEHICLE:

If you are a member of a credit union, I would start there. Then progress to the banks. The dealerships are usually a little higher, so unless they are having a fantastic promotion, I would shop elsewhere for the financing. There are a variety of prices and interest rates out there, so shop around.

You absolutely do not want to have the car financed under the Rules of '78. This is still sometimes used by the banks, so always ask them! The Rules of '78 simply means that you pay all of the interest first, and even if you pay off the vehicle early, you still have to pay all of the interest for the entire period of the loan. Doesn't sound fair, does it?

SOME HELPFUL TIPS WITH PURCHASING ARE:

1. When visiting the car dealer showroom, remember that the salesperson is trained to sell you everything but the kitchen sink. You do not need undercoating, unless you live near the sea shore, because the car already comes undercoated from the factory. Other unnecessary items are fabric protection, rust proofing, and extra service contracts.

2. Never tell the salesperson what you can afford to pay as a monthly payment! This is very important! They will try to work everything around this figure. In other words, "Don't tell me what it costs, just tell me what my monthly payment will be."

3. Don't fall for the dealer's preparation fee, or document preparation fee. This is just another way to put more money in the dealer's pocket.

4. Heaven help you if you decide to take the dealer's financing package, and you enter the finance office. These people go for the jugular vein with no mercy. They can come up with so many things to take your money, you won't even know what happened to you.

5. If you do not get the *Consumer Reports* on the car you want to buy, get a copy of *Edmund's New Car Prices*, which lists base costs of each car and the accessories. Check the prices on the sticker on the window of the car, and this will give you a good idea of the dealer's profit, which is usually about 10-20% higher than cost. *Edmund's New Car Prices* can usually be found at the library.

6. The best time to buy a car is the last day of the month, and the best month to buy is December. By the end of the year, car dealers are scrambling to make deals to reach their quotas and to sell out the previous years models.

7. My personal opinion is that it is better to buy than to lease. You are going to pay about 15% more by leasing, and you still have most all the expenses.

NOW YOU ARE READY TO FACE THE TASK OF SELLING YOUR OWN VEHICLE:

First, there are several ways of finding out what your car is worth, both retail and wholesale:

1. *Consumer Reports Used Car Price Service*: Call (800) 594-9245 for a verbal price on the phone. The fee is $10.

2. Next, you can turn to:

   The Gold Book
   P. O. Box 105068
   Atlanta, GA. 30348
   (404) 847-6500

   You can subscribe to their yearly service, which covers the prices of older vehicles, contemporary cars, and trucks.

Note: Many libraries have this book on hand.

3. Or, you can go to the library and ask for the *N.A.D.A. Official Used Car Guide,* which will tell you what the car is worth if you sell it. Also, you can ask for the N.A.D.A. *Official Wholesale Used Car Trade-In Guide* which will tell you what you would get if you traded it in. Usually, a

good selling price is somewhere in the middle of these two prices.

You may also subscribe to either one of the N.A.D.A. appraisal guides by calling or writing the following if your library does not carry them:

N.A.D.A. Appraisal Guides
P. O. Box 7800
Costa Mesa, CA. 92628-9924
(800) 966-6232

4. And finally, watch the newspapers for the prices people are asking for your type of vehicle.

None of the prices are set in concrete. You must arrive at your own price.

AUTOMOBILE LEASING:

To lease or not to lease? That is the question! Leasing is a very complicated matter, which gives you the privilege of renting a vehicle while still paying for the financing, down payment, depreciation, sales tax or excise tax (depending on your locality), maintenance, cost of repairs over the warranty, etc., etc., And, at the end of the lease, you have no equity—no vehicle!

It is suggested that you compare all benefits and liabilities of both owning and leasing to determine which is best for you. It is my personal opinion that leasing is best left to businesses instead of individuals.

Essentially, the purpose of this book is to get you out-of-debt, and leasing is just another liability you would be assuming, with no benefit at the end. Pros and cons for leasing are listed hereafter for your consideration:

PROS:

1. Your monthly payment may be lower. If no down pay-
    ment was required, your monthly payment will be a few
    dollars more, since you are in effect financing the down
    payment.

2. No hassle with a trade-in or selling a car at the end of the
    lease.

3. Allows you to drive a more expensive car than you can
    really afford, and to replace the car more often.

CONS:

1. When the lease is up, you have no equity and no vehicle.
    You have to start all over again, or buy the vehicle at the
    leasing company's inflated price.

2. Leasing is generally more expensive than buying.

3. Early termination of a lease results in severe penalty.

4. You still have to pay for repairs not covered by the war-
    ranty.

5. You must still pay the expenses as if you had purchased;
    i.e., sales tax or excise tax (depending on your locality),
    maintenance costs, property tax (if that applies in your
    jurisdiction), and auto insurance.

6. At the end of the lease, other penalties may be applied for
    the following:

    Extra mileage charge over the specific allowance
    (usually 12,000 miles per year).

    Excessive wear and tear.

    Any damage to interior, or exterior body.

See the SUGGESTED READING section for more information.

INSURANCE—CONFUSION, FRUSTRATION OR WHAT:

HOW MANY DIFFERENT TYPES OF INSURANCE DO WE CARRY, AND WHAT TYPES OF INSURANCE ARE NOT NEEDED?

Insurance has always been very difficult for me to understand, and if you have ever tried to read your policies, I am sure you will agree.

Have you ever told an insurance agent what you want in general terms; i.e., Homeowners Insurance, and left it to the agent to make sure that you received the best policy? Later, when some mishap occurred and you filed a claim, you find out too late that you were only covered for depreciated value of the item instead of *replacement* value! How very frustrating this can be! You have been faithfully paying the premium thinking you were totally protected. Make sure you check with your agent and give them hypothetical "what if" situations to answer. Don't take everything for granted.

Never buy the following types of insurance! They are tremendously inflated in price. You just plain don't need them if you are already covered under a hospitalization policy and a life insurance policy, which we will discuss below:

- Credit Life Insurance
- Mortgage Life Insurance

- Credit Card Loss & Theft Protection Insurance
- Specialty Health Insurance that covers only one disease; i.e., cancer

You do not need credit life insurance and mortgage life insurance. Simply make sure you are sufficiently covered with your life insurance policy to pay off the debts of mortgage, autos, installment loans, funeral expenses, and what your family will need to live on after you are gone. If you are not sufficiently covered, then increase your coverage.

Credit card loss and theft protection insurance is totally unnecessary! Earlier we discussed that the law limits your liability if you report the loss or theft within two days. This is just another gimmick by the banks to take your money.

If you have a Hospitalization Policy, you certainly do not need another policy that will cover only one disease, when your hospitalization policy covers most all of them.

Also, for your information, if you have an automobile policy, you may not need to buy insurance when you rent a car. Check with your agent about this one. Auto rental insurance is big income to the rental company.

HEALTH INSURANCE:

If you pay for your own hospitalization, you can cut your cost by raising your deductible. If your present deductible is $250, consider raising it to $500 or $1,000. This could save you up to $1,500 a year.

Note: If your family has serious health problems, you will have to give careful consideration to whether or not you want to do this.

LIFE INSURANCE— WHOLE LIFE VERSUS LEVEL TERM LIFE:

How much life insurance should you carry? Do not just pull a number out of the air. Give it some thought, and consider the following:

- Go over all present debt.

- How much is owed on all mortgages?

- Funeral Expenses.

- Children's future needs; i.e., braces, college, special needs provisions.

- Living provisions for your spouse, and family, in the transition period of living without you.

Note: A simple rule of thumb may be five-seven times your current salary.

WHOLE LIFE INSURANCE:

Whole life insurance is very expensive! One reason is that it accumulates cash value and is permanent insurance. There is a much higher commission paid to the salesman on this insurance versus term life insurance.

If you are healthy and insurable, redeem the whole life policy, but ONLY AFTER YOU HAVE APPLIED FOR AND RECEIVED IN HAND YOUR NEW POLICY FOR LEVEL TERM INSURANCE.

LEVEL TERM
LIFE INSURANCE:

Level term insurance is the most economical type of life insurance you can carry. Level term simply means the price and the coverage stays the same for a certain period of time; i.e., 10 years, 15 years, or 20 years. If you purchased a 10-year level term policy for $250,000, the premium stays the same for 10 years and your coverage stays the same for 10 years. It does not decrease as does regular term. Term life does not accumulate cash value and is temporary insurance. Always ask if it can be converted to whole life at the end of its term. This is very important if you are getting older. The savings between whole life and term life can be substantial. However, at the end of the term you have selected, the insurance ceases unless it is a renewable-convertible policy. Before buying, you must ask if it is renewable and convertible to whole life at the end of the term. This is very important! You do not want to be left without insurance at a time in your life when you may need it most.

EXAMPLE: Non-smoking male, age 45, in good health, $250,000 of insurance coverage.

WHOLE LIFE: $4,140 annual premium

LEVEL TERM LIFE:
   10 year $ 347 annual premium
   15 year $ 402 annual premium
   20 year $ 497 annual premium

Note: A savings of from $3,643. to $3,813 annually by changing to a level term life policy.

HOW DO YOU FIND THE LOWEST COST FOR TERM INSURANCE?

There are several services that will do searches of data bases on insurance companies to give you quotes of the least expensive insurance companies. There is no fee for this service:

> MasterQuote
> (800) 337-5433
>
> Wholesale Insurance Network
> (800) 808-5810
>
> Quotesmith
> (800) 556-9393
>
> SelectQuote
> (800) 343-1985

DISABILITY INSURANCE:

Few of us think of the possibilities of being disabled, or that we could lose all that we worked so very hard to obtain. The cost of this protection, if not provided by your employer, could be as follows for a Non-Smoker, Male, 45 years of age and in good health.

EXAMPLE: Income Protection for a $60,000 income: Approximate annual cost of $1,750 would provide for a $3,300 monthly income if disabled. A waiting period may apply.

UMBRELLA LIABILITY INSURANCE (EXTENDED PERSONAL LIABILITY COVERAGE):

This is probably the best insurance you could give your family. In this litigation-happy world we live in, you never know when you are going to be the victim of a lawsuit.

For an umbrella liability policy, the annual cost is about $225 for $1,000,000 in protection. You cannot afford to be without this policy! Get your auto and homeowners insurance from the same company for this to apply, and you may be able to get a discount on the premiums.

HOW DOES IT WORK?

EXAMPLE:

1. Your homeowners policy gives you coverage of $100,000 per occurrence. Someone is hurt on your property and sues you for $500,000, which the court awards. Your homeowners policy will pay $100,000 only, and then your umbrella policy will cover the difference of $400,000.

2. This same scenario covers your auto policy as well. If you are in an auto accident and are sued and the court awards the plaintiff $500,000. Your auto policy pays its limit of $100,000 then your umbrella policy picks up the difference of $400,000.

If you have any property at all, you can be a target for lawsuits, and the umbrella liability policy is your best protection. It actually acts like another policy on top of your homeowners and auto policies, just like an umbrella. It is extra protection over and above your homeowners and auto policies.

AUTOMOBILE INSURANCE:

Here again, *raise your deductibles!* If you increase your comprehensive and collision deductibles from $200 to $500 you can save up to 25-30%.

• If you are driving an older vehicle that is worth less than $1,000-$1,500 in value, cancel the collision and comprehensive coverage. If you are in an accident, your insurance company is not required to fix your vehicle; instead, they can pay you what they assess your vehicle to be worth, and after the deductible, there is almost nothing left.

- Ask for senior discounts, if applicable; good driver discounts; and multiple vehicle discounts if you are insuring more than one vehicle.

- Cancel the death, dismemberment and loss of sight provision. You are already covered with your hospitalization and term life insurance policies. The odds of losing just your sight in an accident is not that great.

- Shop prices with several companies as premiums vary greatly.

- All of the above are just ways of making your agent richer. Have you ever gotten your policy and found you had coverage you never ordered?

- You will save anywhere from $150 to $900 depending on how many of the above steps you follow and the age of your vehicle.

- For general questions about insurance, call the National Insurance Consumer Helpline at (800) 942-4242.

UNNECESSARY AND DUPLICATED INSURANCE— CANCEL THESE OVER-PRICED FORMS OF INSURANCE:

- CREDIT CARD LOSS AND THEFT INSURANCE— Earlier you filled out the form listing all credit card companies, addresses, phone numbers and credit card numbers. Keep this list in a safe place and remember you are only liable for $50.00 on each card, if it is reported within two days of loss. This is the law, so you don't need additional insurance. It is just another profit center for the banks.

- CREDIT LIFE INSURANCE—If you have made some major purchases (TV, appliances, etc.) and the sales-person asked you to buy credit life insurance, remember if you are carrying sufficient level term life insurance to pay off all debt and expenses, etc., you don't need this very inflated insurance on one item.

- MORTGAGE LIFE INSURANCE—This goes along the same lines as credit life insurance. Again, if you have suf-ficient life insurance, you don't need mortgage life insur-ance. Keep in mind that mortgage life insurance normally decreases in value, so the longer you have it, the less it is worth.

- EXTENDED WARRANTIES—Think of how many times you were sold an extended warranty on something you purchased! Was it a television, or an appliance? How many times did you actually make a claim? I thought so-not very many times, if at all.

  Extended warranties are very, very profitable sources of income for the seller. I once bought an extended war-ranty on a refrigerator, and later found out the warranty only covered one part! What a waste!

HOSPITALIZATION INSURANCE:

DO NOT CANCEL—But, if you pay your own hospitaliza-tion, consider raising the deductible.

If you raise your $250 deductible to a $500 or $1,000 deductible, you will save a significant amount of money.

Simply call your agent, and have them give you a quote. You will be amazed at the savings.

A word of caution here—If you or your family has a history of continuous sickness, this may not be advisable. You be the judge here.

LIFE INSURANCE:

Assuming that you are insurable, and that you have in hand your new level term life insurance policy, then it is time to cancel whole life, variable life, and universal life insurance.

Note: If you are not insurable or are in your later years, do not cancel your whole life policies. The older you get the higher your premiums are going to be and you may not be insurable after your level term policy expires. This is very important.

We previously reviewed the difference between level term insurance and the whole life products, so we will not go over them again here.

Once you have applied for your level term life insurance and you have been approved and the POLICY HAS BEEN ISSUED, and you have it physically in your possession, then and only then, cancel any whole life policies you may have and get the refund of the cash value.

Once you have received the **Cash Value Refund,** I know it will be very tempting to go out and spend it on everything in sight, but please refrain from doing that. Keep your eye on your main objective of paying off all debt. Therefore, apply that refund first to credit card debt, then to any other installment type of debt such as autos, etc. If there is anything left after all other debt is paid, then apply the balance to your mortgage as we will show you in the next chapter, or you to put this aside for a start on your 3 months of cash living expenses. This will be your cushion in case of unexpected and emergency expenses.

WHAT A RELIEF THIS ONE CHANGE CAN MAKE IN YOUR LIFE! HOW ABOUT IT?

CHAPTER 5

WHAT IS YOUR PRESENT FINANCIAL CONDITION?

HOME MORTGAGES:

THERE IS A WAY OUT OF THIS DEBT TRAP many, many years earlier than scheduled. The answer is very simple, and we will look at that solution in just a moment.

Statistics show that only 9% of the population retire with over $50,000 income per year. Keeping that figure in mind, after paying taxes of about 50% (per our previous exercises), there is only $25,000 left to pay your mortgage and all remaining living expenses. How then can you afford to have a mortgage? The picture gets much darker if you are one of the 91% who did not retire with $50,000 or more income. It certainly behooves us to pay off our mortgage at the earliest possible date.

If you are a homeowner with a mortgage, when you went to the settlement table you were handed a "Truth In Lending Statement" that showed you were going to pay a total of $315,929 for that $100,000 house you are buying. The attorney told you to just sign it and not pay any attention to that $315,929 figure because your payment is only going to be $878 principal and interest. Was the $315,929 figure an error? No! If you pay by the bank's terms for the 30 years to pay-off, you will pay $315,929 for that $100,000 house!

No investment in the country (that I know of) can come close to touching the rate of return of paying off your mortgage early! Your home is your greatest investment. Now consider this return. Your monthly payment of principal and interest only, is $877.58, and is broken down as Interest of $833.33 and $44.25 of principal. By *pre-paying* that month's principal of $44.25, you have saved yourself $833.33 of *future interest*. That equals a *369%* return on your money! Now compare that to the stock market, or any other investment you can image! Your best investment is going to be your own debt. Invest by paying it off early.

I hear so many times from people that if they pay off their mortgages, they will lose most of their tax deductions! While this is true on one hand, you have to look at the whole picture to see the total benefit.

For example, say you have a mortgage interest deduction of $10,000 and you are in the 28% income tax bracket. You had to spend the $10,000 in order to save the 28% tax, or $2,800. In other words, you just *lost* $7,200!

	$10,000.00	paid in mortgage interest
	- 2,800.00	saved by the write-off of interest at 28% rate
Bottom Line	$ 7,200.00	Lost—You could have used this for vacation!

IMPORTANT NOTE:

If you want tax deductions, start your own business! This is an excellent suggestion, and one you should consider. I did! Even part-time will give you many tax advantages.

The choice is yours! You can pay the banks way and throw away thousands upon thousands of dollars, or you can do it my way, and save thousands and thousands of dollars. Which would you rather do? Order an amortization schedule from your lender on your present loan, and you can see that in the first ten years of your mortgage, 90-92% of your payment goes to interest.

Also, according to your amortization schedule from your lender, you can see that it takes about 22-24 years before 50% of your payment goes to principal. What could you be doing with an extra $50,000 or $100,000 or $150,000 or more that you did not have to pay to the bank in the form of interest?

Note: If you do not want to obtain an amortization schedule from your lender, you can purchase a book entitled, "Monthly Interest Amortization Tables" published by Contemporary Books. You can verify the percentages quoted above.

Eradicate that mortgage by paying it off early! Here's how:

When you went to settlement on your mortgage loan, you also signed a note agreeing to re-pay the loan and giving the terms and conditions of re-payment, which was probably a FNMA/FHLMC Uniform Instrument Note. CHECK YOUR

NOTE TO BE SURE THAT YOU HAVE THE RIGHT OF
PREPAYMENT WITHOUT PENALTY.

Item Number 4 of this document should show your
rights of prepayment as follows:

"4. BORROWER'S RIGHT TO REPAY

I have the right to make payments of principal at any
time before they are due. A payment of principal only is
known as a 'prepayment.' When I make a prepayment, I will
tell the Note Holder in writing that I am doing so."

HOW MUCH SHOULD YOU PRE-PAY AND WHEN?

First, call your mortgage company and ask them to send
you an Amortization Schedule for your loan. Some lenders
charge for this service, and others do not, so ask. This Amortization Schedule will show you a breakdown of each payment as to how much goes to principal and how much is
applied to interest throughout the full term of the loan.

Second, find out where you are on the Amortization
Schedule; i.e., what is your present balance, and what is the
next scheduled payment due. You are now going to make
your regular monthly payment, and in addition, you are
going to write out a separate check for the next month's*
principal only, (as shown on your amortization schedule),
and on that check you are going to write "APPLY IMMEDI-
ATELY & DIRECTLY TO PRINCIPAL ONLY ON LOAN
#_____." You may wish to write a separate note to the
lender advising the same information. In this case, write out
your note and make copies of it so all you have to do is fill in
the blanks each month.

Also note that you can make an additional payment of
principal only in whatever amount you wish. The drawback

is that you will not know your exact balance unless you calculate it each month.

Remember, you can make as many future payments of principal on one check as you want.

Third, next month, you will again make your full regularly scheduled payment. If you have the funds to make an extra payment or so, feel free to do so, but if you do not have the extra funds that month, it makes no difference. You do not have to make an extra principal payment.

It is very important to keep in mind that each month you have to make a *full* payment of principal and interest, no matter what! By making extra principal payments, this does *not* allow you to skip a month with no payment at all! You must fulfill the terms of your Promissory Note each and every month, and that requirement is a full payment of principal and interest.

Now, what happens if you do not tell the lender in writing where and when to apply your extra payments? The lender has four choices. They can apply those funds to anyone of the following:

*1. Apply directly to the principal of the loan.

*2. Apply your payments to the last payment of your loan

*3. Put your payments in an escrow account.

*4. Or, put your payments in an account entitled, "Unapplied Funds."

If you were the bank and making the profit off this loan, where would you apply the extra payments? Make sure you know how your extra payments are being applied. Check up on the bank!

---

* *Source:* Mortgage Management Systems, Inc.

The benefit of making your extra principal payments in the exact amount of your next month's principal portion of the payment as shown on your Amortization Schedule is that you know exactly what your balance is and exactly how much interest you have saved! This is very easy to keep up with, and avoids the hassle of not knowing what you owe after you have made an extra payment. For instance, if you just pull a figure out of the air for say $50 or $100 and you make this as your extra principal payment, how are you going to know what your balance is or how much longer you have to go on your loan without tremendous math calculations?

This is a very simple method and will allow you to pay off your mortgage loan years early. Depending on how many extra principal payments you make, you could pay off a 30-year loan in 7, 10, 15, or 20 years. Not only that, you can add up all that interest on your prepayments, and tell exactly how much you have saved in interest. Remember, if you saved all that interest by making prepayments of principal, you did not have to earn all that money you would have paid in interest!

We will leave the subject of mortgages with this last thought. What could you do with the money you make if you did not have to make that mortgage payment?

IS THERE A YELLOW BRICK ROAD TO FINANCIAL FREEDOM?

You bet there is, and it is called *knowledge!* Knowledge in turn will give you *power.* We have to know what is wrong before we can fix it.

In the pages that follow, we are going to explore our present income & expenses on a monthly basis, as well as expenses that are due quarterly, semi-annually, and annually.

We are going to take the first step right now, and that is to determine our present *installment debt.*

Now, please refer to Form C-1, CURRENT DEBT PROFILE.

List all of your revolving and installment debt; i.e., credit cards, bank loans, auto loans, student loans, etc. Anything you are making payments on right now. Do *not* include the mortgage here. Fill in the Type of Debt, Present Balance, Amount of Monthly Payment, and Interest Rate.

Now get your calculator and we are going to go through some simple math calculations for each debt.

1. Divide your monthly payment into the present balance and write that figure in the column entitled, Approximate Number of Months to Pay Off. Note: For this exercise, we are not even going to look at the interest. This is only to give you an idea of how fast you can pay off your debts.

2. We now have the number of months it would normally take us to pay off the debt, *not* including the interest. Now go to the Position of Payoff column, and we are going to rank the debt in order of priority of payoff. Place a 1 beside the least number of payments due, a 2 beside the next least and a 3 beside the next until you have finished the list.

3. You now have the order and priority of payoff for each debt shown. You are going to pay off Number One first, then Two, then Three, on down the list.

4. If your #1 bill for payoff is the first item of $500, and your minimum payment is $25 per month, it would normally take you 20 months to pay it off, not including the interest.

5. We are now going to find some extra money to add to this payment. This is not as hard as you may think. We all spend money without thinking or adding it up. For instance, I used to buy a specialty coffee and a pastry every morning, which normally cost me about $4.25 a

CURRENT DEBT PROFILE
Form C-1

Debt Name	Type of Debt*	Interest Rate	Present Balance	Amount of Monthly Payment	Approx. No. of mos. to Payoff	Position of Payoff
VISA	C	16.9%	$500	÷ $ 25	= 20	1
MasterCard	C	12.5%	$1,000	÷ $ 30	= 28	2
Auto Loan	A	8.75%	$6,000	÷ $200	= 30	3
Bank (2nd Trust)	H	12.5%	$5,000	÷ $112	= 60	4
				÷	=	
				÷	=	
				÷	=	
				÷	=	
				÷	=	
				÷	=	

* I=Installment, C=Credit Card, A=Automobile, E=Education, H=Home Equity

day. $4.25 times 20 days a month, and I had spent $85.00 in one month that I could have put toward a bill. When I realized what I was doing, I started taking my breakfast with me each morning. This was not the only seemingly insignificant thing I spent money on, and I am sure that you can come up with a few things you can live without as well.

6. Keep a log of everything you and your family spend your money on for a month, and then separate this into categories of food, transportation, etc. This will be quite an eye opener for you, and will enable you to make the necessary adjustments to your spending and lifestyle which will allow you to re-direct some extra money each month to help pay off existing debt. See SUGGESTED READING.

7. Back to the payoff of Item #1 of $500 with a $25 minimum payment. We are going to say that you can come up with an extra $100 each month. We are going to add that to the $25 we have to pay anyway, and now we are going to pay $125 each month until this debt is paid off, which should take four months instead of 20 months with the minimum payment.

8. Once you have paid off Item #1, move to Item #2, a $1,000 debt with a minimum payment of $30. We are going to roll the $125 we were paying on Item #1 into the payment on Item #2 of $30, so we are now going to pay $155 per month on this debt. How did we arrive at a $155 payment? During the payoff period of four months for Item #1, we were still paying the minimum payment of $30 on Item #2; therefore, the balance is now $880. We are now going to pay $155 per month on this debt until it is paid, so it will be paid off in just six months.

9. We now go to Item #3 on our list. Since we started this program, we have been making payments of $200 per

month for 10 months, now leaving a balance on Item #3, of $4,000. We are now going to roll over the extra $155 we were paying from Items #1 & #2 into the payment for Item #3, so we will now pay $355 per month. This debt will be paid off and gone within 11-12 months.

10. Now we move to Item #4, and since starting the program, we have made 22 regular payments of $112 which now leaves a balance to be paid of $2,536. We now take the $355 extra money and add to the $112 minimum and we will now pay $467 per month until all is paid in 6 months.

What have we accomplished here? Per the regular payment schedule, it would have taken *five years*, or 60 months to pay off all this debt. We have paid off the entire debt in less than half the time—*only 28 months*. Now it is time to put away 3 months savings for living expenses and emergencies before we start paying the mortgage.

From this point on, you will take the extra $467 and apply it to your mortgage loan as principal only payments, which we have previously discussed. Go back to the mortgage pay off section and you can now calculate using your Amortization Schedule, when you will own your home, completely free of debt.

I think you can now get the picture of just how easy this program can work. It is extremely important that you do not go back to the old habits, of charge, charge, charge. It will be very easy to do, so you must discipline yourself to follow the pay-off steps, and stay out of future debt. We will talk later about how to find extra money to accomplish our extra payments.

To help you understand and conquer why you or your spouse are compelled to spend, please refer to SUGGESTED READING.

WHAT IS YOUR PRESENT FINANCIAL CONDITION?

- You have to get a picture in your own mind, and on paper, of just what your present financial condition is; where it is good, or where it is in need of extensive help.

  Roll up your sleeves and take about 30-60 minutes to fill out the financial forms that follow. You will find blank forms for your use in the back of this book. All forms are self-explanatory.

  Start with the PERSONAL FINANCIAL STATEMENT, *Form C-2.*

  This form will show you exactly what you are worth today. In other words, if everything were to be liquidated today, what would you have left? Add up all your assets, and subtract all of your liabilities, and this will equal your net worth.

- Next, fill out the VARIABLE EXPENSE ANALYSIS *(Form C-3).*

  Here you will list only expenses that occur at specific times of the year; i.e., quarterly, semi-annually, annually.

  Add up the total yearly expenses and then divide by 12. This will give you the amount of money you must save per month to handle all those unscheduled expenses. Put this money into a savings account or something that will give you immediate access to your funds. Put this money aside each month as if you were paying a bill.

  This monthly figure will be needed when you fill out *Form C-5,* ACTUAL MONTHLY CASH FLOW ANALYSIS, and *Form C-4,* MONTHLY INCOME & EXPENSE ANALYSIS.

PERSONAL FINANCIAL STATEMENT
Form C-2

_____
Date

ASSETS	LIABILITIES
Cash:	Real Estate Mortgages: _____
On Hand _____	_____
Checking Accts. _____	
Savings Accts. _____	Notes Payable:
	To Banks - Secured _____
Listed Securities: _____	To Banks - Unsecrd. _____
	To Relatives/Others _____
Unlisted Securities: _____	
	Accounts & Bills Due: _____
Accounts & Notes	
Receivable _____	IRS Taxes Due: _____
Retirement Plans: _____	Other Unpaid Taxes: _____
	Loans Payable:
_____	Automobiles _____
Real Estate Owned:	Education _____
(Market Value) _____	Life Insurance _____
	Credit Cards: _____
_____	_____
Real Estate Mortgages	_____
Receivable: _____	
Life Insurance:	Other Debts: _____
(Cash Value) _____	_____
Annuities _____	
Personal Property:	**TOTAL ASSETS** _____
Automobiles _____	
Boats/Tractors _____	**LESS TOTAL**
Furnishings _____	** LIABILITIES** _____
Other Assets: _____	**EQUALS NET WORTH** _____
_____	

VARIABLE EXPENSE ANALYSIS
Form C-3

DESCRIPTION	YEARLY COST	WHEN DUE Annual, Semi-Annual, Quarterly
DENTIST	_____	_____
DOCTORS	_____	_____
CLOTHING	_____	_____
GIFTS:		
Birthday/Anniversary/Holiday	_____	_____
Flowers	_____	_____
Contributions-Charities, Etc.	_____	_____
DUES & SUBSCRIPTIONS:	_____	_____
INSURANCE:		
Life	_____	_____
Automobiles	_____	_____
Home Owners	_____	_____
MAINTENANCE & REPAIRS		
House	_____	_____
Automobiles	_____	_____
Grass	_____	_____
TAXES:		
Real Estate	_____	_____
Personal Property	_____	_____
County/City Vehicle Decals	_____	_____
Licenses	_____	_____
IRS	_____	_____
Accountant	_____	_____
Estimated Income Tax Deposits	_____	_____
VACATION:	_____	_____
OTHER (Itemize)	_____	_____
TOTAL	_____	÷ 12 = _____ /mo.

- Now go to the MONTHLY INCOME AND EXPENSE ANALYSIS, *Form C-4*

In this form, we will assess our financial health at the end of the month. Will we have a surplus, or will we need to cut expenses in order to avoid a deficit?

Income should be shown net; the amount you actually bring home after taxes, etc. have been taken out by your employer.

List all expenses that you anticipate for the month, as well as the figure you arrived at on *Form C-3* to cover your variable expenses for one month.

Take your total net income and subtract your total expenses. This shows the final result for the month. If your income is more than your expenses, then place a plus (+) in front of the final figure. If your expenses are more than your income, then place a minus (-) in front of the final dollar figure.

- The Next form to be filled out is the ACTUAL MONTHLY CASH FLOW ANALYSIS *(Form C-5)*.

- Having already filled out the Monthly Income & Expense Analysis, you now know how much income is coming in per month, and what your expenses are for the same period of time. We are now going to use these figures to work through *Form C-5*, ACTUAL MONTHLY CASH FLOW ANALYSIS.

This form simply breaks down the month into two halves. You will list everything that comes *due for payment* between the first of the month and the 15th in the first column, and everything that comes due between the 16th and 31st of the month in the second column.

If you are paid twice a month, put the date you *receive your pay* at the top of the first column, and the same for the second column. If you are paid weekly, just include the first two pays in the first column, and the second two pays in the second column.

This is something that you will do each month, as this is your guide to where you are in the month. It will show you what

MONTHLY INCOME AND EXPENSE ANALYSIS
Form C-4

INCOME:
    NET (Take Home) Salaries   _____
    Commissions   _____
    Dividends/Interest   _____
    Other   _____
        TOTAL NET INCOME   _____

EXPENSES:

HOUSING:		CHILDREN:	
Mortgage/Rent	_____	Child Care	_____
Telephone	_____	School Tuition	_____
Electricity	_____	Lessons	_____
Gas	_____	Supplies	_____
Water/Sewer	_____	Allowances	_____
Cable TV	_____		
		CLOTHING	_____
INSTALLMENT DEBT:		CHARITY:	_____
Credit Card	_____		
Credit Card	_____	RECREATION:	_____
Credit Card	_____		
Auto #1	_____	MEDICAL/DENTAL/	
Auto #2	_____	DRUGS	_____
Education	_____		
Other	_____	FOOD:	_____
TRANSPORTATION			
Gasoline	_____	COSMETICS/ETC.	_____
Buses/Rail	_____		
Car Pool	_____	OTHER: (Itemize)	_____
Other	_____		
INSURANCE		TOTAL EXPENSES	_____
Life	_____		
Dental/Vision	_____	NET INCOME	_____
Health	_____	LESS EXPENSES	_____
Other	_____	SURPLUS/DEFICIT	_____
		(+ or -)	

ACTUAL MONTHLY CASH FLOW ANALYSIS
Form C-5

Month of	October	15th	31st
		Date of Pay	Date of Pay
INCOME FROM ALL SOURCES		2,500	2,500
EXPENSES			
MORTGAGE/RENT		1,200	
UTILITIES:			
ELECTRIC		87	
GAS OR OIL		55	
SEWER/WATER			22
CABLE TV		43	
CREDIT CARD & LOANS			
VISA		100	
MasterCard			75
Auto Loan			243
TRANSPORTATION:			
GASOLINE/OIL			105
BUS/RAIL/TAXI		25	25
FOOD		200	200
LUNCHES		120	120
PERSONAL CARE		25	25
CHILD CARE/EXPENSES		240	240
MEDICATIONS/VITAMINS			30
CHARITY		50	50
MISCELLANEOUS			
Newspapers			18
VARIABLE EXPENSES			
Life Insurance			200
Auto Insurance			245
TOTAL EXPENSES		2,145	1,598
SUBTRACT EXPENSES FROM INCOME FOR SURPLUS OR DEFICIT (+ OR -)		+ 355	+ 902
CARRY FORWARD TO NEXT MONTH		(+ or -)	+ 1,257

bills are coming up for payment, and how much money you are going to need in order to pay them.

These financial forms will help you get control. You will have to study them over and over again during the month. This will help to reinforce in your mind what you are trying to do, and will show you immediately from month-to-month exactly what you have accomplished!

This is your *road map*. Stick with it!

You may make copies of the forms for your own personal use only. There are blank forms in the back of this book.

After filling out all of these forms, I know that many of you are now totally depressed after seeing the results. Don't be too discouraged, because there are ways you can dig up some extra money to which you already have access. We will review these options just a little later in the very next chapter.

But first, we will take a brief look at credit reports.

CREDIT REPORTS: VIEW AND HAVE ERRORS CORRECTED!

There are about 16 different credit reporting companies throughout the U.S. but we are just going to look at the top three:

EXPERIAN (FORMERLY TRW)
P. O. Box 2104
Allen, TX. 75013
(800) 392-1122

EQUIFAX
P. O. Box 105873
Atlanta, GA. 30348
(800) 685-1111

TRANSUNION CORP.
P. O. Box 390
Springfield, PA. 19064-0390
(216) 779-7200

- If you have been declined employment, credit, or insurance due to a credit report within the last 30 days, you can get a free copy of your report by writing a letter. Call the phone numbers listed above, and a recording will give you a listing of the information you must supply in your letter of request.

- If you just want to check your report, Experian (formerly TRW) will give you a complimentary copy, but only one a year. The others will charge between $8.00 to $16.00.

- Get all errors corrected! Each credit reporting company may have different information on you, and that includes different errors. Therefore, it is best to check all three companies to make sure their information is correct.

Errors are very easy to make. You may have the same last name of another individual, and maybe your first initials are the same, but they stand for different first names. There are many ways a credit reporting company can make a mistake, so make sure you check your report with each company.

This is especially important if you decide that you want to get a lower rate credit card or home equity loan, in order to pay off those high rate credit cards.

Keep in mind that in the future when the banks are all paid off, and all debts are gone, you won't need the banks anymore. You will have the money to finance your own projects yourself!

CHAPTER 6

STEPS TO PUTTING MONEY BACK INTO YOUR POCKETS

WHERE DO WE GET THE EXTRA MONEY TO PAY OFF OUR DEBTS FASTER?

ELIMINATE UNNECESSARY SPENDING:

ACTUAL MONTHLY EXPENSES—Keep track of every penny you and your family spends. Once you see in black and white *how* you have been spending your money, you will be able to pick out the expenses that can be eliminated. See SUGGESTED READING.

Remember my illustration of stopping by the coffee shop each morning? By making my breakfast at home, I saved $85.00 per month. I am sure that you can come up with many more ways to save money.

We have to stop kidding ourselves! You have the power to choose: Either to continue on as you have done in the past, or to turn over a NEW LEAF and get out of debt! The choice is yours! You will lose your chance for a debt-free tomorrow if you continue as you have done in the past. Believe me, I know. Yesterday is gone. Let it go, and grab onto the new day, as it is just beginning!

WHAT MOTIVATES OUR BAD SPENDING HABITS?

- Lack of training in handling money from our parents, and following in their footsteps as well as those of other relatives and friends. This is no time to follow the crowd! You must now march to the sound of your own drummer!

- Depression—Spending makes us feel better until the bills arrive.

- Feelings of anger, hurt, disagreements with a spouse and children, boss and co-workers.

- Boredom—Bored with life, career, and lifestyle.

- Envy—Envious of other people's lifestyles, and wanting to play "catch-up."

- Children—Trying to fulfill all of their wants, even when we know we cannot afford to do it. I remember saying, "I don't want my children to do without as I did."

- Unhappiness—With our present job, boss, co-workers, spouse, family & life.

- Free time—Too much of it can get you into trouble!

- Struggling—In an unfulfilling or bad relationship.

- The "I haven't done anything for me lately" syndrome. Feeling sorry for ourselves. This one will always get us in trouble.

- Childhood—The patterns learned as a child can be among the most devastating of all. These patterns can be changed, and in many of us, they must be changed, or you may not be able to resist getting back into debt again even if you conquer the overwhelming feat of becoming debt-free. So many people once they have paid off a credit card, feel a surge of freedom, and instead of directing that feeling into paying off another credit card, they will go right out and charge again. So you can see how very important it is to conquer the old patterns now. You can refer to the SUGGESTED READING list in the back of this book for some good sources of help.

I could go on and on, but I think your are getting the picture. Remember, the choice is yours!

CHAPTER 7

INCREASE YOUR INCOME

Here are some suggestions:

INCOME TAX REFUND:

If you normally get an income tax refund each year, make a vow to yourself to *never again* go out and spend this money foolishly! You *must* apply these funds to your debt according to our previous ranking of priority of pay-off; i.e., credit cards first, then installment loans such as automobiles, furniture, student loans, etc., until you reach the big one, the mortgage.

This is not "found" money. It is your hard earned cash which you can now put to work for your financial future! Please don't shoot yourself in the foot by spending these funds on things you would just like to do or buy. An income tax refund can sometimes make a huge dent in your debt load.

Another alternative, but one that I don't usually recommend, is that you can raise your number of tax exemptions to give you a little more money with each pay check.

You can normally raise your exemptions by one for each $600 you received in your refund. This will not amount to very much money, and if you are the type of person who will spend every cent you get, then do not do this. Your only salvation may be that income tax refund each year!

YARD SALES:

Everyone has stored and unused items everywhere. Take the time to go through the closets, attic, basement, storage sheds, etc. and pull out things that you don't use, or don't anticipate using. Pull out those clothes that the children have out-grown along with old toys and baby furniture, if you are not going to use them again. Pull out old tools, bicycles, lawn mowers or anything that you can do without. Keep in mind that one person's junk is another person's treasure!

You may want to join together with several of your neighbors or a whole community for a community yard sale, which usually brings in more buyers.

This is an immediate source of income to you, and can provide the money you need to get a jump start on your debt elimination system, or just provide you with the few dollars that means you can play catch-up on some over-due bills.

When I made my last move, my Yard Sale brought in $1,200 in just one weekend. I was thrilled, to say the least. Don't under-estimate the power of this vehicle for quick, quick money.

TURN YOUR HOBBY INTO A MONEY-MAKING VENTURE:

Every one of us has something that we just love to do. Maybe just to help us relax and take our minds off the work day and problems. And just maybe, you are very good at this hobby. This could be an excellent opportunity to teach others how to do exactly what you do. You can charge by the hour, or by the class, or by the course. This is something you can do in your home, or at a community center, school, etc. You may even be able to teach for some other organization or community program. Your opportunities here can be endless. Just put your thinking cap on to see just where your talents really lie. You may have special expertise in cooking, sewing, painting, faux marbelizing wall treatments, painting pictures, crafts, stained glass, woodworking, writing, and so on.

If any one of the above is one of your hobbies, I am sure that you already have a place where you work on them in your home, so what you will have to focus on is getting your product before the public so it can be sold. You may want to contact local retail stores or consignment shops and arrange to place samples with them and take orders, or just consign the item for sale.

Earlier I told you about my doll-making business when I was fourteen years old. I made my samples and took them to several beauty salons and asked them to take orders for me, which they did. You can give the shop owner a portion of the profit, or agree on a price per item. I knew that the ladies who visited the salons to get their hair done each week had children at home or better yet, grandchildren who would love to have one of my dolls. The dolls were placed at the cash register, so there was ample time for the ladies to ask questions about the dolls while paying their salon bill. This little venture allowed me to buy my own clothing, and supply my own needs for school and modeling courses, etc., so from the time I was fourteen years old until I left home, my mother and father only had to provide me with food and a roof over my head.

PART-TIME EMPLOYMENT:

If you just need to make ends meet, or you need a little something extra coming in to get started on your debt-reduction program, you may want to consider taking a part-time job to get you over the hump. This could be a job that would take you outside of your home, or something you could do at home, like baby-sitting or doing the grocery-shopping, or running errands for sick, elderly, or handi-capped people. If you have a computer, you may want to consider doing free-lance word processing.

RENT OUT A ROOM OR TWO:

My Grandmother survived the 1928 Flu Epidemic which killed nearly 50% of the town, including my Grandfather. She had two little children and was pregnant with the third when my Grandfather died a young man at the age of 28. She survived by renting out rooms in her home.

When I lost everything to the bankers, was unemployed, and had very little money in my pocket, I rented a house and sub-let two of the rooms; one for $400/month, and the smaller one for $375 plus one-third of the utilities.

A word of caution, however. Be sure you thoroughly check out the individual(s) you are considering as a tenant(s). Ask for references from former landlords and call them! Get a security deposit of one month's rent, as well as the first month's rent in advance! Be careful to whom you rent. Keep in mind also that you will lose some of your privacy. Taking in a tenant is a big step, so think about it carefully. Be sure you lay down the ground rules to your new tenant before renting, so that they have an opportunity to either accept or reject those rules. Remember, it is your house.

Renting out a room in your home can bring in anywhere from $300 to $500 per month extra income, plus pay part of your utilities. Of course, the amount you can charge will be based upon your location and home. Look in the classifieds in the newspaper to determine what others are charging in your area.

SELL SOMETHING YOU DO NOT USE:

Men have to have bigger toys than women do and these items usually get stored away and used very little. No offense, fellas! Let me give you an example.

I know someone who was bitten by the fishing bug, and had to have their own bass boat. They would not buy a used boat. They had to have a brand new boat, which cost about $6,000. They have had this boat in the back yard now for about five years, and have only used it three times! Why? Because they do not have time. They would have been better off to have just rented a boat for those three fishing trips, which they could have done for about $50 per trip, or a total of $150.

Does it really make sense to spend all that money when you don't have it? To finance the boat, and pay all that interest? Those three fishing trips were the most expensive they ever took!

At present, I have not been able to convince this individual to sell the boat, but if they did, they could probably get about $3,500 for it. This would be a good nest egg for someone who is struggling to make ends meet, or get out of debt.

Give this concept some serious consideration. Put pride

of ownership on the back burner and see what a difference this could make in the life of your family. There are many other items that can be considered as well, such as an extra vehicle that is not being used, or a set of golf clubs, or a piece of jewelry, or furniture.

BECOME A PREDATOR ON THE TRACK OF WASTEFUL SPENDING:

Gigantic rewards will be reaped if you will take the time to track your spending for at least one month! If you have ever asked yourself the question, "Where does my money go?", you will surely find out if you faithfully keep track of every penny you spend. In the meantime, here are some ideas to help you stretch the dollars that you already have.

RESTAURANTS AND EATING OUT:

Eating out is a favorite past-time in this country, and I must admit, I was one of those individuals who ate out several times a week. Until I really got serious about getting out of my own debt, I really never stopped to see how much it was actually costing me. Wow, what a surprise! I was spending hundreds of dollars on this favorite activity! Now I am not saying to stop eating out entirely, but I am saying to cut back to a reasonable level. You don't have to go cold turkey, but if you eat out 3–4 times a week, then cut it back to once a week. Also consider how much each of you eat. Instead of bringing home half your dinner in a doggie bag, split a dinner and order an extra salad or baked potato.

PACK YOUR LUNCH:

If you have to get out of the office or away from the job on your lunch hour, pack your lunch and go sit on a park bench, or somewhere quiet. Take a good book with you, and allow yourself to unwind. Eating lunch out has gotten to be as expensive as dinner used to be. What a tremendous savings when you pack your lunch.

PASS UP THE SPECIALTY COFFEE HOUSE:

Earlier I shared with you my addiction to the specialty coffees. Each morning I would go in and get my coffee and a roll or muffin, and hardly ever got out of there for under $4.00. When I stopped, I was saving between $75—$85 a month on something so small. I know time is a rare commodity for almost everyone, but take a minute to make your own coffee and cereal at home, and take it with you if you need to.

GIVE UP ONE OR MORE OF YOUR VICES:

Drinking and smoking are two of the most common vices. Giving either of them up may be easier said than done, but if you have the will, you will find the way! Just look at how much healthier you will be, and this can really be a place where you can save some big bucks. If you are a smoker, add up the amount you spend each year on cigarettes. You could probably pay off a credit card or two with the money you spend here!

BARTER YOUR SERVICES:

Take an inventory of your abilities and talents, and barter your services with someone who needs those services and who can likewise provide you with something you need. It may be baby sitting, typing, carpentry, etc. You can trade services or even goods, like a piece of furniture. Use your imagination. The point is that you need to start looking for ways *not* to spend money.

GIFTS:

Give gifts of personal service, or something you have made instead of purchased gifts from a store. Most people will appreciate your personal touch, especially if your gift takes into consideration the needs of the person.

RECYCLE AND GET PAID FOR IT:

When I was a teen, I used to gather up aluminum cans and newspapers, and take them to the local recycling center. They would weigh my goods and pay me so much per pound.

CLEAN YOUR OWN HOUSE:

Cleaning your own house or apartment will save some serious money, and it is good exercise. I was paying $240 a month to a housekeeping service. What a dent that would make in your debt reduction plan!

GROCERY SHOPPING:

Do your shopping in stores where you can bring your own bags and load your own groceries in your car. The savings in the prices charged will definitely surprise you.

CHAPTER 8

STOP IMPULSIVE SPENDING

- Lock up all credit cards.

- Analyze present lifestyle and adjust to "below your means."

- Analyze the bad habits that make you spend.

LOCK UP ALL CREDIT CARDS:

Take those pieces of plastic and *lock them up!* Get them out of your reach, and make it difficult to get hold of them. This will virtually eliminate all impulsive buying, because you will not be able to buy more than you can pay for in cash. It will force you to *think* and *think again.* You will have to *plan* to spend instead of spending before you plan. A student in one of my seminars shared his own method for resisting impulse buys. Although I think this may be just a little drastic, it does bring a laugh. He thought it would be hard for him to get to his credit cards if he froze them in ice in the freezer! He reasoned that by the time the cards had thawed, his reason for spending would probably be gone. I do not recommend that you take this solution seriously!

ANALYZE YOUR LIFESTYLE:

Far too many people in this country are spending away their future. On average, we spend about 110–115% of every dollar we make. It does not take a rocket scientist to see the end result of this behavior.

Analyze your present life style and make adjustments to live *below your means,* instead of above it. You do not have to keep up with the neighbors, your siblings, or your friends. Take pride in your own accomplishments and in yourself.

If your analysis shows that you are living in a home you cannot afford, then make some very tough decisions about that situation. If practical, sell it and move to something you can afford. We keep trying in our lives to get everything bigger and bigger, and better and better, whether we can afford it or not. Believe me, I know about this one. I lost my 14,000 square-foot house.

This can also apply to fancy cars, club memberships, entertainment, or whatever. Pride is our biggest enemy on this one. We worry about what everyone will think if we start scaling down? Who cares what they think! This is your future, and believe me, you will be in a much better position to put on a show if you are debt-free. Think about it!

ANALYZE BAD SPENDING HABITS:

Take a minute here and sit down and list those habits that may have gotten you to spend needlessly. What are your motivations and weaknesses? Take into consideration your spouse and any other family members, and their influence upon you and on the family spending. You must sit down and go to self-confession. Once you realize why you are over-spending, you can begin to correct the habit. Again, see SUGGESTED READING for more help here.

DON'T LET YOUR SPOUSE LEAD YOU ASTRAY:

Once you have started on this new path to become debt-free, don't let your spouse or other family members lead you astray. Don't let this happen to you. Everyone will be whispering in your ear; especially your kids, who can come up with some real good ideas for spending money.

Make your children aware of the goal, and make sure they understand what this will mean to their future. Give small rewards when they achieve an accomplishment in not spending, whatever it may be.

You can help yourself overcome temptations before they arise by writing little notes to yourself to encourage and up-lift. Put them where you can easily see them every day; i.e., on your bathroom mirror, the sun visor of your car, on your checkbook, in your daily calendar, etc. Use your imagination, and you will come up with some very innovative creations.

DON'T GO TO PLACES THAT TEMPT YOU TO SPEND:

Stop reading the sale ads for department stores or any other store where you are tempted to shop. I used to sit down with the Sunday newspaper, and the first thing I would look for was the advertising. All this does is tempt you, because you may see one or two things that really interest you and you will go running to the store and come out with several things you had not even considered or needed. This is the whole psychology of marketing. They have to get you in the store, and once there, you will spend, spend, and spend some more!

Break this cycle by not even reading the ads. You can do it! Believe me, if I can do it, so can you.

Gravitating to the shopping malls or stores when you are hurt, depressed or angry is by far the worst thing you can do for your financial health. When you are in this state of mind, you are more likely to spend and absolutely waste your money on anything that comes into view. My remedy for this follows:

I have gotten all the way to the shopping mall and parked the car. With my hand on the door handle and just about to step out of the car, I have stopped and asked myself the following three questions:

1. Do I really need this item, or anything in this store or mall?

2. Will I use the item if I buy it?

3. Do I have the money in cash to pay for it now?

The answer to all three questions, was "no!" I would just be trying to fill a need that I was experiencing for something else. I would then argue with myself, and after convincing myself that I did not have the money or the need, I would start the car and go home. With this accomplishment under my belt, I would pat myself on the back the whole way home for overcoming the useless urge to spend!

STOP DOING WHAT YOU HAVE ALWAYS DONE:

If you put a note on your sun visor with the above three questions on it, this will help tremendously. Before you get out of the car, put down the sun visor and ask yourself those questions. We have to break old habits if we are going to succeed. Congratulate yourself when you have conquered your spending urges.

Doing what you have always done has gotten you into heaps of trouble before. If you don't stop, you will be in worse condition next year than you are today!

STOP PROCRASTINATING:

It only takes 21 days to change a habit—good or bad! Take the first step and do it now. Don't put it off another minute. Get on with it! The road to a financially free life is not all that long.

BUY NECESSITIES FROM DEPARTMENT STORES ONLY AT END-OF-SEASON:

Never pay the department store prices, and one way around this is to shop their END-OF-SEASON sales. Almost all merchandise is put on sale at some point in the year.

My mother was a master at this, because she had to make what little money we had stretch as far as it would go. I remember each January and July she would make her trips to the department stores for their linen sales to buy sheets and towels. On December 26th she would be the first in line to buy next year's Christmas cards and ornaments, gift wrap, ribbons, and small appliances. After all, the biggest selections and bargains were immediately after Christmas when the stores sold this extra inventory at rock-bottom prices. I learned a lot from my mother!

SENIOR CITIZENS DISCOUNTS:

Depending on your age, there are many discounts available to you. Always ask if a place or organization gives a discount and at what age. This can be anywhere from 50 years to 65 years and older. Just ask, if you fall within this age range.

Most restaurants give Senior Citizen Discounts of 5% or 10%. Not to mention the airlines. Here you can really hit a bonanza if you are the proper age. I have several friends that fall into this category, and I am always astounded at the bargain-basement prices they pay.

CHAPTER 9

BECOME A THRIFTY SHOPPER

- Buy an older vehicle (One or two years old)
- Clip coupons
- Do meal planning and advance cooking
- Attend auctions
- Look for things you do need to buy at Yard Sales first
- Buy wholesale wherever possible
- Join discount buying organizations
- Shop at consignment shops
- Buy from department stores only at end-of-season

- Take advantage of senior citizen discounts

- Check the discount travel brokers if your have to make a trip

- Find low-cost or no-cost entertainment for you and your family

Stop throwing your money away! You can become a thrifty shopper and get your money's worth. You can learn to be thrifty and stretch your money as far as it will possibly go.

If you are interested in a subject, learning can be loads of fun. I have always told my children that if you want to know something, there is bound to be a book on the subject somewhere. I have always found this to be true. No matter what I have wanted to know, someone has written a book about it. Read several books on the subject so that you get a clear perspective from several authors.

Some ideas are listed below to help you get started on becoming an investigative sleuth who uncovers areas of wasteful spending. Refer to the SUGGESTED READING section for other ideas:

BUY AN OLDER VEHICLE:

Let someone else take the beating in depreciation on a brand new car. Buy a car that is one or two years old, with *low mileage.* A car that has been cared for can give you many years of good service. You can find them in the newspaper, through a friend, or through a friend of a friend. Someone always knows someone else and what they have to sell. If someone is about to trade-in their present car for a new one, you can offer them $500 more than they would get for their trade, and it would be a good deal for both of you. A dealership is only going to give them a wholesale price for their trade. You can also check with banks about their repossessed vehicles.

CLIP GROCERY COUPONS:

I have told you previously not to read the sale ads, but grocery ads are the exception. Discount coupons are offered by manufacturers to promote their products, and are honored by most grocery stores. I have saved up to $12-$15 at a time, just using coupons for products that I buy anyway.

If you are fortunate enough to live in an area where a grocery store offers double and triple coupons, you are very lucky. We have one such store in our area, and the savings can be astounding. If you look at your savings as a percentage of your overall grocery bill per trip, the return can be better than investments in most stocks!

DO MEAL PLANNING AND ADVANCE COOKING:

This will really pay off when you take a good hard look at your grocery bill. By doing your meal planning and cooking for two-week or four-week periods, you will save time and money. This is also very convenient when both spouses work, and meal preparation time is limited. Go to the library and get a book on the subject. Your biggest savings will be in the area of prepared foods. You will no longer be buying loads of convenience foods, because you will already have done your cooking, separated the cooked foods into meal portions, and frozen those meal portions so that you just have to defrost, warm and serve.

AUCTIONS:

Auctions are well worth attending if you have *specific items in mind*. This is *not* a good place to go just for entertainment! It is very easy to get caught up in the thrill of the bid. This is an addiction as well for many people. If you go just for entertainment, you *will* get into trouble.

On the other hand, I have furnished most of my home from antique auctions, and in so doing, I have beautiful antique furniture that is worth far more than I paid. You can furnish a whole house for what you would pay for 1-2 rooms of furniture at the retail stores. When you purchase at auctions, your selections are usually one-of-a-kind and most unique.

YARD SALES AND FLEA MARKETS:

Don't pass up the flea market or yard sale. You just don't know what bargains you can come away with at a cost of maybe .10 cents to .25 cents on the dollar. Many things are brand-new, or barely used.

One of the benefits of flea markets and yard sales is that you can bargain for the best deal. Most people are willing to negotiate. Remember, I previously stated that one person's junk is another person's treasure. It just depends on the need.

The yard sale is an excellent place to find baby and children's clothing and accessories, exercise equipment, etc. Sometimes, you can even find a treasure, when someone sells something without having any knowledge of its worth; i.e., a vase or piece of silver that has been handed down through the family and one of the spouses does not like it. I purchased a piece of coined silver at a flea market for $25.00. I checked the inscription on the bottom, and found that instead of sterling, as I had thought, it turned out to be coined, which is much more expensive. I sold the piece for $250.00. I also purchased a brand new full-size bicycle for $15.00 that was still in the original box and had never been taken out and put together. If you have priced bicycles lately, you know that was a real buy.

If you do not have the money for auctions, and you are handy at refinishing, this is also a good place to buy old antiques and strip them down and refinish them so they look brand new. I could go on and on, but I think you get the point.

BUY WHOLESALE WHEN POSSIBLE:

Never pay retail again! This is possible for many of your needs. There are many companies that sell exclusively wholesale, including mail-order catalogs. You can find them in the newspapers, yellow page telephone directories, and the local library.

The library is usually your best source for information. If you do not know how to locate the information yourself, ask the librarian to help and instruct you. This is their job, and they are glad to help. Libraries carry books and listings of just about everything. I have rarely come out of a library empty-handed, or without a referral to somewhere else.

You will also find some ideas in the back of this book under SUGGESTED READING.

JOIN DISCOUNT BUYING CLUBS AND ORGANIZATIONS:

There are many organizations which offer discounts to members on a variety of products and services. For instance, the AAA (American Automobile Association) and AARP (American Association of Retired Persons) offer some of the following:

- Discounts on hotels
- Discounts on airline and railroad fares, cruises, and tours.
- Discounts on auto rentals

- Insurance

- Auto repairs

- AAA offers trip planning services, road maps, and even reservation services.

There are also different clubs and cooperatives which allow you to stretch your dollar further. For instance, there are food-buying clubs that you can join. In some areas, people have gotten together and created a cooperative food-buying service. I get my electric service from an electric service cooperative. With this I get back capital credit refunds, which is cash or credit back to me. Here again, the possibilities are numerous.

SHOP AT CONSIGNMENT SHOPS:

Do your day-to-day clothing shopping at a nice consignment shop. Shop around until you find one that carries good quality clothing, and not just junk. You will be able to find many things that are brand new, or almost new, and you will be able to buy clothing for about a quarter of what you would pay at the department store.

In my area, I have found an upscale consignment shop carrying many designer labels. I have paid $59.00 for a designer outfit that originally cost $600.00 Not bad for just a little shopping!

You never know where you can get a discount, so always ASK! Ask at department stores, movie theaters, beauty salons, restaurants, etc. What discounts they offer and to whom. Remember, you probably will not get it unless you ask!

DISCOUNT TRAVEL BROKERS:

If you need to take a trip somewhere, check with the discount travel brokers first. Many are listed in the newspaper (some good and some bad, so ask around). If you are flexible in the time you can travel, you can get some real deals. For instance, about 2-3 weeks before a scheduled tour is to leave, if it is not full, they will discount the same tour just to fill the seats. You may be able to get a tour from $350—$500 that someone else has already paid $1,000 for and they paid months earlier. Sometimes it pays to wait and to be flexible.

FIND LOW-COST ENTERTAINMENT FOR YOUR FAMILY:

If you live in a Metropolitan area, it will be easier to find more no-cost entertainment than it will be in a rural area. However, it does not make any difference where you live, because a rural area will offer different forms of entertainment that will still be just as much fun.

If you and your family enjoy going to the movies, many theaters offer discounted prices during certain times or on special days. Check all theaters in your area for their prices and discounts. I was astonished to find two theaters in my area that offer $1.50 seats anytime, and another at $3.25 seats anytime. Another theater offers $4.50 seats any day up to 6:00 P.M. Be sure you check with the theaters periodically because they may change their pricing without notice.

Be sure you eat before you go so you are not tempted to throw away your hard-earned money at the popcorn stand. You will pay through the nose here. If they are discounting the movie, then they are going to make it up on the popcorn stand which they know most people cannot resist. If you must have something to eat at the movie, take it with you; such as, a candy bar, peanuts or something small that you can put into a purse or pocket. The theaters do not like you to bring your own food for obvious reasons. If you are tempted to buy at the popcorn stand, just remember, this is one of the most expensive foods you will put in your mouth.

Hobbies can be turned into an excellent form of entertainment and weekend trips for very little or no cost. Here
are some ideas:

- GENEALOGY—I have only recently discovered this
  wonderful and exciting pastime. It is so interesting to
  find out about your ancestors. You may find some out-
  standing accomplishments or some ordinary ones. But
  the process is so much fun. We have discovered several
  Civil War relatives and some from the American Revolu-
  tionary War, and we have been taking trips to various
  battlegrounds and cemeteries to find lost relatives. All
  this generally starts with a family Bible, or stories from
  one of your oldest living relatives. This is something the
  whole family can get involved in and enjoy. Take a picnic
  lunch and enjoy the countryside.

- EXERCISE—Exercise is something we all need, but our
  way of life turns most of us into couch potatoes. You can
  create healthy competition in the family with a little inge-
  nuity. Don't forget to buy your exercise equipment at a
  yard sale for the best price!

- FAMILY GAMES AND SPORTS—Take inventory of
  what you and your family like to do, and organize some
  games. It may be a board game, bird watching, exercise
  or skating. Make it something you enjoy.

- CONCERTS AND SPECIAL EVENTS—Look in your
  newspaper for free events and concerts. Most of these
  will be in the evening or on the weekends.

- LIBRARIES—Create family interest in things that are in
  your own backyard, or perhaps something you found on
  one of your trips. It could be a special type of rock
  formation, a new little creature you have never seen
  before, or a beautiful bird. Whatever it may be, go to the

library and make it a project for the whole family. It can be anything from looking into what makes it rain, to learning why the sun comes up each morning. Here again, the ideas can be endless.

- VISIT PARKS—Parks are wonderful places to go on the weekends for an outing with the family. There are all kinds of parks to choose from including city, county, state and national parks. Historical parks are perhaps the most interesting as history comes to life before your eyes. This can be a tremendous help to your children in their school classes as well.

- MUSEUMS—There are museums for just about anything you can think of. A museum is a walk back into history, and a place where the whole family can learn and benefit.

I am certain you can come up with many more ideas. These few suggestions are offered to give your mind a slight boost off the diving board.

CHAPTER 10

YELLOW BRICK ROAD TO FINANCIAL FREEDOM

EXCITING TIMES AWAIT YOU AS YOU put this plan into action! No more waiting for The Prize Patrol to knock on your door with $1 million in prize money! No more waiting for your lottery number to hit. With odds of 7.1 million to 1, this is not a good investment.

DEVELOP THE MILLIONAIRE MINDSET—COMPOUND INTEREST:

Did you know that if you invested as little as $100 or $200 a month on a consistent basis, you would be a millionaire! Take a look at *Figure 5* below. This chart assumes a 12% return on your money.

COMPOUND INTEREST INVESTMENT

Monthly Investment	Yield	No. of Years	You Would Have Invested	Now Worth
$ 100	12%	40	$ 48,000	$1,188,242
$ 200	12%	35	84,000	1,299,054
$ 500	12%	25	150,000	948,818
$1,000	12%	20	240,000	999,148

Figure 5

As you can see from the chart, the earlier you start, the better off you will be with the least amount invested. Becoming a millionaire is not difficult, it just takes consistent effort. It is so easy!

You now have a road map to financial freedom, and keep the following in mind:

SET YOUR GOALS:

Each day, make out a written list of the things you want to accomplish that day, and then rank them in order of priority. Start with number one and go down the list until you have completed them. Do not skip around. Finish number one before you start number two. If you do not finish the list, that is fine. Just move the unfinished items over to the next day's list and continue on day-to-day. By writing down what you need to do, you will accomplish about 10 times more than what you would normally have done without a written list.

KEEP FOCUSED:

Remember, *inch-by-inch it's a cinch!* Keep your mind on your ultimate goal to be debt-free! Don't get discouraged. You did not get into this situation overnight, and you are not going to get out of this overnight either.

BECOME A CONTRARIAN:

You will have to become a contrarian to accomplish your goal. You cannot continue to do what the crowd continues to do; i.e., going out and increasing your debt and living from paycheck to paycheck. For you, it will no longer be chicken one day and feathers the next. No more feast or famine, only debt-free living and freedom to do what you want, when you want. If you have no debt, and your cars are paid for, and your home is paid off, then no one can take them away from you, can they?

PLUG INTO THE SOURCE:

It is hard to accomplish such a huge task without plugging into a higher source. For me, that source is God. You may call it something else. That source can help you over the tough spots in the road and give you the inner strength to continue on to attain your ultimate goal. Don't try to do it all alone. Remember, even the Lone Ranger had Tonto!

Your Yellow Brick Road to Financial Freedom will encounter some bumps and pot holes. Just keep your eyes on your dreams. Don't look back at the old; look ahead to your debt-free future. Sit back and just begin to imagine how it will feel when all debt is gone.

KNOWLEDGE IS POWER!

Your Yellow Brick Road is knowledge. Below is a blueprint, and all you have to do is apply it to your own finances:

- Determine your present financial condition
- Figure out your monthly expenses and income
- Determine where the extra money will come from
- Make out a time-table for pay-off of all debt
- Cancel duplicated and unneeded insurance and collect your refunds
- If insurable, change from whole life to level term life insurance
- Eliminate unnecessary expenses
- Break the old habits of spending
- Never pay retail again
- Pay off all credit card and installment loans, including automobiles
- Save 1-3 months living expenses to carry you through any problems in the economy. With all installment debt now paid off, it will be easier to put some money aside to give you a cushion against unexpected expenses. If you do not have a cushion to fall back on in times of unexpected problems, you could be forced back into the same debt position you had before. Put this money aside before you start paying off the mortgage.

- Pay off home mortgages.

- Start investing for retirement, and fun

CONCLUSION:

I shared with you earlier a motto that has helped me to get on with it, and you may want to adopt it as well:

"IF IT'S GOING TO BE, IT'S UP TO ME!"

Awe-inspiring power is felt when you have accomplished your first goal, and then your second; until your debts are paid off one-by-one! I don't know that I can truly explain the feeling; the increase in self-confidence and self-esteem, the exuberance of power you feel in controlling your own destiny.

The warning lights are flashing, "Rocky Shore Ahead." It is your choice to ignore the warnings, or to do something about it.

THE CHOICE IS YOURS!

CHAPTER 11

BLANK FORMS

HOW MUCH OF YOUR INCOME
DOES THE TAX MAN REALLY TAKE?
Form A-1

	ONE YEAR	45 YEARS
INCOME:	_____	_____
LESS TAXES:		
Federal Income Tax (28.00%)	_____	_____
State Income Tax (5.75%)	_____	_____
Soc. Sec. & Medicare (7.65%)	_____	_____
State Sales Tax—multiply your gross income x 33% (1/3 is an estimate of your disposable income), and then multiply by the sales tax rate for your state: (4.5%)	_____	_____
Real Estate Tax—take from your tax bill	_____	_____
Personal Property Tax —from your tax bill	_____	_____
TOTAL TAXES	_____	_____
Income after major taxes**	_____	_____

The total of all taxes divided
by gross income equals your
effective rate of tax: _____ %

(You are paying a whopping _____ to your various government bureaucrats!)

Note: We have not included self-employment tax, federal
excise taxes on cigarettes, gasoline, etc.

CREDIT CARD ANALYSIS
Form B-1

Credit Card Name or Number:				

Grace Period:
   None
   25 days
   Other				

Billing Cycle:
   24 days
   30 days
   What day of the month
   does the cycle start				

Annual Fee:
   None
   How Much				

Balance Transfer from
Other Credit Cards:
   When does the interest
     start accruing?
      Day of Transfer
      Next Cycle
 	
   Is there a surcharge
   for the transfer - how much
 	
   Is the transfer treated as a
   Cash Advance - What is the
   interest rate				

Cash Advances:
   What is the interest rate
   Does the interest rate start
   immediately				

Interest Rate:
   Is it a special offering rate
   and for how long - What is that
   rate
   Fixed Rate - What is it
   Variable rate				

Late Payment Fee: How much				

NOTE: Refer to your monthly statements or initial offering information to fill out this form.

CREDIT CARDS EMERGENCY CONTACT LIST
Form B-2

Card Name & Address	Phone # to Report Loss	Account Number	Who Carries This Card*
_____ _____ _____ _____	_____	_____	_____
_____ _____ _____ _____	_____	_____	_____
_____ _____ _____ _____	_____	_____	_____
_____ _____ _____ _____	_____	_____	_____

H = Husband, W = Wife, B = Both, O = Other _____

CURRENT DEBT PROFILE
Form C-1

Debt Name	Type of Debt*	Interest Rate	Present Balance	Amount of Monthly Payment	Approx. No. of mos. to Payoff	Position of Payoff
				÷	=	
				÷	=	
				÷	=	
				÷	=	
				÷	=	
				÷	=	
				÷	=	
				÷	=	
				÷	=	

* I=Installment, C=Credit Card, A=Automobile, E=Education, H=Home Equity

PERSONAL FINANCIAL STATEMENT
Form C-2

_____
Date

ASSETS	LIABILITIES
Cash:	Real Estate Mortgages: _____
On Hand _____	_____
Checking Accts. _____	
Savings Accts. _____	Notes Payable:
	To Banks - Secured _____
Listed Securities: _____	To Banks - Unsecrd. _____
	To Relatives/Others _____
Unlisted Securities: _____	
	Accounts & Bills Due: _____
Accounts & Notes	
Receivable _____	IRS Taxes Due: _____
Retirement Plans: _____	Other Unpaid Taxes: _____
_____	Loans Payable:
	Automobiles _____
Real Estate Owned:	Education _____
(Market Value) _____	Life Insurance _____
_____	Credit Cards: _____
Real Estate Mortgages	_____
Receivable: _____	_____
Life Insurance:	Other Debts: _____
(Cash Value) _____	_____
Annuities _____	
Personal Property:	**TOTAL ASSETS** _____
Automobiles _____	
Boats/Tractors _____	**LESS TOTAL**
Furnishings _____	** LIABILITIES** _____
Other Assets: _____	**EQUALS NET WORTH** _____
_____	

VARIABLE EXPENSE ANALYSIS
Form C-3

DESCRIPTION	YEARLY COST	WHEN DUE Annual, Semi-Annual, Quarterly
DENTIST		
DOCTORS		
CLOTHING		
GIFTS:		
Birthday/Anniversary/Holiday		
Flowers		
Contributions-Charities, Etc.		
DUES & SUBSCRIPTIONS:		
INSURANCE:		
Life		
Automobiles		
Home Owners		
MAINTENANCE & REPAIRS		
House		
Automobiles		
Grass		
TAXES:		
Real Estate		
Personal Property		
County/City Vehicle Decals		
Licenses		
IRS		
Accountant		
Estimated Income Tax Deposits		
VACATION:		
OTHER (Itemize)		
TOTAL		

$\div 12 =$ _____ /mo.

MONTHLY INCOME AND EXPENSE ANALYSIS
Form C-4

INCOME:

NET (Take Home) Salaries   _____

Commissions   _____

Dividends/Interest   _____

Other   _____

TOTAL NET INCOME   _____

EXPENSES:

HOUSING:		CHILDREN:	
Mortgage/Rent	_____	Child Care	_____
Telephone	_____	School Tuition	_____
Electricity	_____	Lessons	_____
Gas	_____	Supplies	_____
Water/Sewer	_____	Allowances	_____
Cable TV	_____		
		CLOTHING	_____
INSTALLMENT DEBT:		CHARITY:	_____
Credit Card	_____		
Credit Card	_____	RECREATION:	_____
Credit Card	_____		
Auto #1	_____	MEDICAL/DENTAL/	
Auto #2	_____	DRUGS	_____
Education	_____		
Other	_____	FOOD:	_____
TRANSPORTATION			
Gasoline	_____	COSMETICS/ETC.	_____
Buses/Rail	_____		
Car Pool	_____	OTHER: (Itemize)	_____
Other	_____		
INSURANCE		TOTAL EXPENSES	_____
Life	_____		
Dental/Vision	_____	NET INCOME	_____
Health	_____	LESS EXPENSES	_____
Other	_____	SURPLUS/DEFICIT	_____
		(+ or -)	

ACTUAL MONTHLY CASH FLOW ANALYSIS
Form C-5

Month of _____

	Date of Pay	Date of Pay
INCOME FROM ALL SOURCES		
	=====	=====
EXPENSES		
MORTGAGE/RENT		
UTILITIES:		
ELECTRIC		
GAS OR OIL		
SEWER/WATER		
CABLE TV		
CREDIT CARD & LOANS		
_____		
_____		
_____		
_____		
TRANSPORTATION:		
GASOLINE/OIL		
BUS/RAIL/TAXI		
FOOD		
LUNCHES		
PERSONAL CARE		
CHILD CARE/EXPENSES		
MEDICATIONS/VITAMINS		
CHARITY		
MISCELLANEOUS		
_____		
VARIABLE		
_____		
_____		
_____		
TOTAL EXPENSES		
	=====	=====
SUBTRACT EXPENSES FROM INCOME FOR SURPLUS OR DEFICIT (+ OR -)		
CARRY FORWARD TO NEXT MONTH (+ OR -)		=====

CHAPTER 12

SUGGESTED READING

THE BEGINNING:

- *A Monetary History of the United States,* by Milton Friedman & Anna Schwartz, Publisher, National Bureau of Economic Research

- *None Dare Call It Conspiracy,* by Gary Allen and Larry Abraham, Publisher, Buccaneer Books, Cutchogue, N.Y.

- *The Prize, The Epic Quest For Oil, Money & Power,* by Daniel Yergin, Publisher, Simon & Schuster

MONEY PSYCHOLOGY:

- *Money Harmony: Resolving Money Conflicts in Your Life and Relationships,* by Olivia Mellan, Publisher, Walker and Company

- *Overcoming Overspending, A Winning Plan for Spenders and Their Partners,* by Olivia Mellan, Publisher, Walker and Company

- *The Money Drunk,* by Mark Bryan and Julia Cameron, Publisher, Ballantine Books

MONEY SAVINGS:

- *1001 Ways to Cut Your Expenses,* by Jonathan D. Pond, Publisher, Dell Publishing

- *Great Buys for People Over 50,* by Sue Goldstein, Publisher, Penquin Books

- *Penny Pinching: How To Lower Your Everyday Expenses Without Lowering Your Standard of Living,* by Lee and Barbara Simmons, Publisher, Bantam Books

- *The Underground Shopper,* by Sue Goldstein, Publisher, Andrews, McMeel & Parker

- *The Wholesale-by-Mail Catalog,* by The Print Project, Publisher, Harper Perennial

- *Wholesale Guide to Buying Furniture,* by Home Decor Press

MAGAZINES:

* *Best Fares Discount Travel Magazine* (800) 880-1234 (40%-75% off on flights and hotel accommodations)

NEWSPAPERS:

* *The Spotlight Newspaper,* 300 Independence Ave., S.E., Washington, D. C. 20003, (202) 546-5621

MONEY TROUBLE:

* *Money Trouble: Legal Strategies to Cope with Your Debts,* by Robin Leonard, Published by Nolo Press

SOFTWARE:

* EXPERT LEASE PRO: Chart Software, P.O. Box 145, Gilman, IL. 60938

(Ask about computer systems requirements.)

MONEY TRACKING:

* *Where Does the Money Go? Taking Control of Your Personal Expenses* by Andy Mayer, Published by W.W. Norton & Company.

* *The Money Tracker* by Judy Lawrence, Published by Dearborn Financial Publishing, Inc.

Your Notes

Appendix

NATIONAL FOUNDATION OF CONSUMER CREDIT

MEMBER AGENCIES

Note: Most member agencies operate under the name of Consumer Credit Counseling Service

ALABAMA

Anniston, CCCS of Central Alabama	1-888-260-2227
Anniston, ADD Credit Counseling	(205) 238-8580
Athens, CCCS of North Alabama	(205) 232-1331
Birmingham, CCCS of Central Alabama	**(205) 251-1572**
Decatur, CCCS of North Alabama	(205) 238-8580
Dothan, CCCS of Alabama	(334) 712-1992
Enterprise, CCCS of Alabama	1-800-662-6119
Florence, CCCS of North Alabama	(205) 764-0810

Foley, CCCS of West Florida	(334) 943-9190
Gadsden, CCCS of Central Alabama	1-888-260-2227
Huntsville, CCCS of North Alabama	**(205) 533-1904**
Jackson, CCCS of Mobile	(334) 246-9898
Madison, CCCS of North Alabama	(205) 533-1904
Mobile, CCCS of Mobile	**(334) 602-0011**
Mobile, Debt Counseling Service	(334) 433-2488
Montgomery, CCCS of Alabama	**1-800-662-6119**
Monstrose, CCCS of Mobile	(334) 990-8499
Opelika, CCCS	1-800-757-2227
Selma, CCCS of Alabama	1-800-662-6119
Tuscaloosa, CCCS of Alabama	(205) 752-2598

ALASKA

Anchorage, CCCS of Alaska	**(907) 279-6501**
Fairbanks, CCCS of Alaska	(907) 451-8303
Homer, CCCS of Alaska	1-800-478-6501
Juneau, CCCS of Alaska	1-800-478-6501
Seward, CCCS of Alaska	1-800-478-6501
Soldotna, CCCS of Alaska	(907) 279-6501

ARIZONA

Chandler, CCCS Southwest	(602) 246-2227
Flagstaff, CCCS Southwest	1-800-308-2227
Luke AFB, CCCS Southwest	1-800-308-2227
North Phoenix, CCCS Southwest	(602) 246-2227
Peoria, CCCS Southwest	(602) 246-2227
Phoenix, CCCS Southwest	**(602) 246-2227**
Prescott, CCCS Southwest	1-800-308-2227
Tempe, CCCS Southwest	(602) 246-2227
Tucson, CCCS Southwest	1-800-308-2227
Yuma, CCCS Southwest	1-800-308-2227

ARKANSAS

Batesville, CCCS of St. Louis	1-800-966-3328
Bentonville, Credit Counseling of AR	(501) 271-8866
Blytheville, CCCS of St. Louis	1-800-966-3328
El Dorado, CCCS	(501) 862-6677
Fayetteville, Credit Counseling of AR	**(501) 521-8877**
Fort Smith, Family Service Agency - CCCS	(501) 484-0311
Hot Springs, Family Service Agency - CCCS	1-800-255-2227
Jonesboro, CCCS of St. Louis	1-800-966-3328
Little Rock, Family Service Agency - CCCS	(501) 372-4242
N. Little Rock, Family Service Agency - CCCS	**1-800-255-2227**
Paragould, CCCS of St. Louis	1-800-966-3328
Pine Bluff, Family Service Agency - CCCS	1-800-255-2227
Rogers, Credit Counseling of AR	(501) 271-8866
Siloam Springs, Credit Counseling of AR	(501) 524-5642
Springdale, Family Service Agency - CCCS	(501) 521-8877
West Memphis, CCCS of St. Louis	1-800-966-3328

CALIFORNIA

Anaheim, CCCS of Orange County	(714) 547-2227
Antioch, CCCS of East Bay	(510) 686-0266
Arcata, CCCS of the North Coast	**1-800-762-1811**
Atwater, CCCS of Mid-Counties	(209) 723-9982
Auburn, CCCS of Sacramento, Inc.	1-800-736-2227
Bakersfield, CCCS/Kern & Tulare Counties	**(805) 324-9628**
Barstow, CCCS of Inland Empire	1-800-947-3752
Beaumont, CCCS of Inland Empire	1-800-947-3752
Berkely, CCCS of East Bay	(510) 729-6966
Bishop, CCCS of Inland Empire	1-800-947-3752
Burbank, CCCS of Los Angelos	(818) 808-4222
Calexico, CCCS of San Diego	(619) 337-2300
Cameron Park, CCCS of Sacramento	1-800-736-2227
Capitola, CCCS of Santa Clara Valley	(408) 423-0909
Cerritos, CCCS of Los Angelos	(310) 808-4222

Chico, CCCS, Twin Cities	(916) 674-9729
Chino, CCCS of Inland Empire	1-800-947-3752
Chula Vista, CCCS of San Diego	(619) 498-0600
Chula Vista, Credit Counselor's of CA	1-800-947-3752
Citrus Heights, CCCS of Sacramento	1-800-736-2227
Concord, CCCS of East Bay	(510) 686-0266
Corona, CCCS of Inland Empire	1-800-947-3752
Costa Mesa, CCCS of Orange County	(714) 547-2227
Crescent City, CCCS of the North Coast	1-800-762-1811
Culver City, CCCS of Los Angelos	(310) 808-4222
Daly City, CCCS of San Francisco	(415) 788-0288
Delano, CCCS/Kern & Tulare Counties	(805) 725-0199
Dublin, CCCS of East Bay	(510) 833-9444
El Cajon, Credit Counselor's of CA	1-800-947-3752
El Cajon, CCCS of San Diego	(619) 447-5700
El Centro, CCCS of San Diego	(760) 337-2300
Elk Grove, CCCS of Sacramento	1-800-736-2227
Encinitas, Credit Counselor's of CA	1-800-947-3752
Escondido, CCCS of San Diego	(619) 487-0900
Escondido, Credit Counselor's of CA	1-800-947-3752
Fairfield, CCCS of Sacramento	1-800-736-2227
Fallbrook, Credit Counselor's of CA	1-800-947-3752
Fontana, CCCS of Inland Empire	1-800-947-3752
Fort Bragg, CCCS of San Francisco	(707) 961-0193
Foster City, CCCS of San Francisco	(415) 788-0288
Fremont, CCCS of East Bay	(510) 795-6656
Fresno, CCCS of Central Valley	**(209) 454-1700**
Ft. Irwin, CCCS of Inland Empire	(760) 243-5983
Fullerton, CCCS of Orange County	(714) 547-2227
Gilroy, CCCS of Santa Clara Valley	(408) 988-7881
Granada Hills, CCCS of Los Angelos	(818) 808-4222
Grass Valley, CCCS, Twin Cities	(916) 674-9729
Greenfield, CCCS of Santa Clara Valley	(408) 754-6712
Grover Beach, CCCS of Ventura County	1-800-364-2227
Hanford, CCCS of Central Valley	(209) 582-2442
Hayward, CCCS of East Bay	(510) 795-6656
Hemet, CCCS of Inland Empire	1-800-947-3752

Huntington Beach, CCCS of Orange County	(714) 547-2227
Indio, CCCS of Inland Empire	1-800-947-3752
Inglewood, CCCS of Los Angelos	(213) 808-4222
Jackson, CCCS of Mid-Counties	(209) 956-1170
Kingsburg, CCCS of Central Valley	(209) 454-1700
La Mesa, CCCS of San Diego	(619) 447-5700
La Mirada, CCCS of Los Angelos	(213) 808-4222
Lakewood, CCCS of Los Angelos	(213) 808-4222
Lancaster, CCCS of Los Angelos	(213) 808-4222
Lemoore/NAS, CCCS of Central Valley	(209) 454-1700
Livermore, CCCS of East Bay	(510) 833-9444
Lodi, CCCS of Mid-Counties	(209) 956-1170
Lompoc, CCCS of Ventura County	(805) 964-2227
Long Beach, CCCS of Los Angeles	(310) 808-4222
Los Angeles, CCCS of Los Angeles	**(213) 808-4222**
Madera, CCCS of Central Valley	(209) 673-6133
Martinez, CCCS of East Bay	(510) 686-0266
Merced, CCCS of Mid-Counties	(209) 723-9982
Mission Viejo, CCCS of Orange County	(714) 547-2227
Modesto, CCCS of Mid-Counties	(209) 522-1261
Montclair, CCCS of Inland Empire	1-800-947-3752
Monterey, CCCS of Santa Clara Valley	(408) 372-9335
Moreno Valley, CCCS of Inland Empire	1-800-947-3752
Napa, CCCS of San Francisco	(707) 527-9221
National City, CCCS of San Diego	(619) 498-0600
North Highlands, CCCS of Sacramento,	1-800-736-2227
Novato, CCCS of San Francisco	(415) 788-0288
Oakhurst, CCCS of Central Valley	(209) 673-6133
Oakland, CCCS of East Bay	**(510) 729-6966**
Oceanside, CCCS of San Diego	(760) 757-2227
Ontario, CCCS of Inland Empire	(909) 781-0114
Oxnard, CCCS of Ventura County	1-800-364-2655
Palm Springs, CCCS of Inland Empire	1-800-947-3752
Palmdale, CCCS of Los Angelos	(805) 947-2227
Palo Alto, CCCS of Santa Clara Valley	(408) 988-7881
Pasadena, CCCS of Los Angelos	(818) 808-4222
Paso Robles, CCCS of Ventura County	(805) 783-2227

Pomona, CCCS of Los Angelos	(909) 808-4222
Porterville, CCCS/Kern & Tulare Counties	1-800-272-2482
Rancho Cordova, CCCS of Sacramento,	**(916) 638-5037**
Red Bluff, CCCS of North Valley	(916) 528-2227
Redding, CCCS of North Valley	**(916) 223-6908**
Redwood City, CCCS of San Francisco	(415) 788-0288
Ridgecrest, CCCS/Kern & Tulare Counties	1-800-272-2482
Riverside, CCCS of Inland Empire	1-800-947-3752
Riverside, CCCS of Inland Empire	**(909) 781-0114**
Rocklin, CCCS of Sacramento,	1-800-736-2227
Sacramento, CCCS of Sacramento,	1-800-736-2227
Sacramento, CCCS of Sacramento,	1-800-736-2227
Salinas, CCCS of Santa Clara Valley	(408) 754-6712
San Bernadino, CCCS of Inland Empire	1-800-947-3752
San Diego, CCCS of San Diego	**(619) 497-0200**
San Diego, CCCS of San Diego	(619) 487-0900
San Diego/Naval Sub Base, CCCS of San Diego	(619) 497-0200
San Diego, Credit Counselor's of CA	1-800-947-3752
San Francisco, CCCS of San Francisco	**(415) 788-0288**
San Jose, CCCS of Santa Clara Valley	(408) 988-7881
San Luis Obispo, CCCS of Ventura County	(805) 783-2227
San Marcos, CCCS of San Diego	(760) 757-2227
San Pablo, CCCS of East Bay	(510) 236-3481
San Rafael, CCCS of San Francisco	(415) 788-0288
Santa Ana, CCCS of Orange County	**(714) 547-2227**
Santa Ana, CCCS of Orange County	(714) 544-8880
Santa Barbara, CCCS of Ventura County	(805) 964-2227
Santa Clara, CCCS of Santa Clara Valley	(408) 988-7881
Santa Clarita, CCCS of Los Angelos	(805) 947-2227
Santa Maria, CCCS of Ventura County	(805) 964-2227
Santa Monica, CCCS of Los Angelos	(310) 808-4222
Santa Rosa, CCCS of San Francisco	(707) 527-9221
Simi Valley, CCCS of Ventura County	1-800-364-2655
Solana Beach, CCCS of San Diego	(619) 757-2227
South Los Angelos, CCCS of Los Angelos	(213) 808-4222
Stockton, CCCS of Mid-Counties	**(209) 956-1170**
Tarzana, CCCS of Los Angelos	(818) 808-4222

Tehachapi, CCCS/Kern & Tulare Counties	1-800-272-2482
Temecula, CCCS of Inland Empire	1-800-947-3752
Thousand Oaks, CCCS of Ventura County	1-800-364-2655
Torrance, CCCS of Los Angelos	(310) 808-4222
Tracy, CCCS of Mid-Counties	(209) 956-1170
Turlock, CCCS of Mid-Counties	(209) 522-1261
Ukiah, CCCS of the North Coast	1-800-762-1811
Vacaville, CCCS of Sacramento,	1-800-736-2227
Vallejo, CCCS of East Bay	(510) 729-6966
Ventura, CCCS of Ventura County	**(805) 644-1500**
Victorville, CCCS of Inland Empire	1-800-947-3752
Visalia, CCCS/Kern & Tulare Counties	(209) 732-2227
Vista, Credit Counselor's of CA	1-800-947-3752
West Covina, CCCS of Los Angelos	(818) 808-4222
Willits, CCCS of the North Coast	1-800-762-1811
Woodland, CCCS of Sacramento,	1-800-736-2227
Yreka, CCCS of Southern Oregon	(916) 841-1516
Yuba City, CCCS, Twin Cities	**(916) 674-9729**

COLORADO

Boulder, CCCS/Greater Denver	(303) 750-2227
Castle Rock, CCCS/Greater Denver	(303) 750-2227
Colorado Springs, CCCS of Southern CO	**(719) 576-0909**
Cortez, CCCS/Greater Denver	(970) 247-1403
Denver/Downtown, CCCS/Greater Denver	(303) 750-2227
Denver/Bear Valley, CCCS/Greater Denver	(303) 750-2227
Denver/Downtown, CCCS/Greater Denver	(303) 750-2227
Denver, CCCS/Greater Denver	**(303) 750-2227**
Durango, CCCS/Greater Denver	(970) 247-1403
Ft. Collins, CCCS of N CO & SE WY	**(970) 229-0695**
Ft. Morgan, CCCS of N CO & SE WY	1-800-424-2227
Glenwood Springs, CCCS/Greater Denver	(970) 928-0903
Grand Junction, CCCS/Greater Denver	1-800-224-9885
Greeley, CCCS of N CO & SE WY	1-800-424-2227
Highlands Ranch, CCCS/Greater Denver	(303) 750-2227

Longmont, CCCS of N CO & SE WY	(970) 229-0695
Loveland, CCCS of N CO & SE WY	(970) 229-0695
Pueblo, CCCS of Southern Colorado	1-800-798-3328
Trinidad, CCCS of Southern Colorado	1-800-798-3328
Westminster, CCCS/Greater Denver	(303) 750-2227

CONNECTICUT

Danbury, CCCS of Connecticut	1-800-450-2808
East Hartford, CCCS of Connecticut	**1-800-450-2808**
Groton, CCCS of Connecticut	1-800-450-2808
Middletown, CCCS of Connecticut	1-800-450-2808
Milford, CCCS of Connecticut	1-800-450-2808
Stamford, CCCS of Connecticut	1-800-450-2808

DELAWARE

| Dover, CCCS of MD & DE | 1-800-642-2227 |
| Wilmington, CCCS of MD & DE | 1-800-642-2227 |

DISTRICT OF COLUMBIA

| Washington, CCCS/Greater Washington | 1-800-747-4222 |

FLORIDA

Alamonte Springs, CCCS of Central FL	(407) 895-8886
Belle Glade, CCCS/Palm Beach County	1-800-330-2227
Belleview, CCCS of Mid-Florida	(352) 867-1865
Blountstown, CCCS of West Florida	(904) 674-2678
Boca Raton, CCCS/Palm Beach County	1-800-330-2227
Bradenton, CCCS/Florida Gulf Coast	(941) 746-4476
Brandon, CCCS/Florida Gulf Coast	(813) 289-8923
Brooksville, CCCS/Florida Gulf Coast	(352) 754-9675
Cape Coral, CCCS/Florida Gulf Coast	(941) 278-3121
Cape Coral, Credit Counseling of FL	(941) 334-3328

Central Miami, CCCS of South Florida	(305) 893-5225
Coconut Grove, CCCS of South Florida	(305) 893-5225
Coral Springs, CCCS of South Florida	1-800-928-2227
Crestview, CCCS of West Florida	(904) 689-0177
Dade City, CCCS/Florida Suncoast	(813) 585-0099
Davie, CCCS of South Florida	1-800-928-2227
Daytona Beach, CCCS of Central FL	(904) 761-5414
Defuniak Springs, CCCS of West Florida	(904) 892-5234
Eglin AFB, CCCS of West Florida	(904) 678-7726
Fort Myers, CCCS/Florida Gulf Coast	(941) 278-3121
Fort Myers/E, Credit Counseling of FL	(941) 334-3328
Ft. Lauderdale, CCCS of South Florida	1-800-928-2227
Ft. Pierce, CCCS/Palm Beach County	1-800-330-2227
Ft. Walton Beach, CCCS of West Florida	(904) 664-6662
Gainesville, CCCS of Mid-Florida	1-800-245-1865
Hialeah, CCCS of South Florida	(305) 893-5225
Inverness, CCCS of Mid-Florida	1-800-245-1865
Jacksonville, CCCS of Jacksonville	**(904) 396-4846**
Jacksonville Beach, CCCS of Jacksonville	(904) 396-4846
Jacksonville/NAS, CCCS of Jacksonville	(904) 396-4846
Jupiter, CCCS/Palm Beach County	1-800-330-2227
Key West, CCCS of South Florida	1-800-928-2227
Kissimmee, CCCS of Central FL	(407) 895-8886
Lake City, CCCS of Mid-Florida	1-800-245-1865
Lakeland, CCCS of Central FL	(941) 687-2515
Largo, CCCS/Florida Suncoast	**(813) 585-0099**
Leesburg, CCCS of Central FL	(352) 326-9004
Lehigh Acres, CCCS/Florida Gulf Coast	(941) 368-3373
Lehigh, Credit Counseling of FL	(941) 334-3328
Liberty City, CCCS of South Florida	(305) 893-5225
Mariana, CCCS of West Florida	(904) 526-1221
Melbourne, CCCS of Brevard	**(407) 259-1070**
Miami, CCCS of South Florida	(305) 893-5225
Miami (Bethune), CCCS of South Florida	(305) 893-5225
Miami (Opa Locka), CCCS of South Florida	(305) 893-5225
Miami Beach, CCCS of South Florida	(305) 893-5225
Miramar, CCCS of South Florida	1-800-928-2227

Naples, CCCS of Southwest Florida	**(941) 775-6688**
New Port Richey, CCCS/Florida Suncoast	(813) 585-0099
North Miami, CCCS of South Florida	**(305) 893-5225**
Ocala, CCCS of Mid-Florida	**(352) 867-1865**
Okeechobee, CCCS/Palm Beach County	1-800-330-2227
Orange City, CCCS of Central FL	(904) 774-2227
Orange Park, CCCS of Jacksonville	(904) 396-4846
Orlando, CCCS of Central FL	**(407) 895-8886**
Orlando, NTC, CCCS of Central FL	(407) 895-8886
Palatka, CCCS of Mid-Florida	1-800-245-1865
Panama City, CCCS of West Florida	(904) 784-6301
Pensacola, CCCS of West Florida	(904) 452-5101
Pensacola, CCCS of West Florida	**(904) 434-0268**
Perry, CCCS of Central FL	(904) 878-0975
Plant City, CCCS/Florida Gulf Coast	(813) 289-8923
Port Charlotte, Credit Counseling of FL	(941) 743-2227
Port St. Joe, CCCS of West Florida	(904) 784-6301
Port St. Lucie, CCCS/Palm Beach County	1-800-330-2227
Riviera Beach, CCCS/Palm Beach County	1-800-330-2227
Rockledge, CCCS of Brevard	(407) 259-1070
Royal Palm Beach, CCCS/Palm Beach County	(561) 434-2544
Sarasota, CCCS/Florida Gulf Coast	(813) 746-4476
St. Augustine, CCCS of Jacksonville	(904) 396-4846
St. Petersburg, CCCS/Florida Suncoast	(813) 585-0099
St. Petersburg/N, CCCS/Florida Suncoast	(813) 585-0099
Stuart, CCCS/Palm Beach County	1-800-330-2227
Tallahassee, CCCS of Central FL	(904) 878-0975
Tallahassee, CCCS of Tallahassee	(904) 878-0975
Tallahassee/N, Debt Counseling Service	(904) 224-4898
Tampa-Carrollwood, CCCS/Florida Gulf Coast	(813) 289-8923
Tampa, CCCS/Florida Gulf Coast	**(813) 289-8923**
Tampa Heights, CCCS/Florida Gulf Coast	(813) 289-8923
Tampa-USF, CCCS/Florida Gulf Coast	(813) 289-8923
Titusville, CCCS of Brevard	(407) 636-9210
Venice, CCCS/Florida Gulf Coast	(941) 493-3180
Vero Beach, CCCS of Brevard	(561) 562-6512
West Palm Beach, CCCS/Palm Beach County	**1-800-330-2227**

GEORGIA

Albany, CCCS of Southwest Georgia	**(912) 883-0909**
Americus, CCCS of Southwest Georgia	(912) 883-0909
Athens, CCCS of Greater Atlanta	1-800-251-2227
Atlanta, CCCS of Greater Atlanta	(404) 527-7630
Atlanta, CCCS of Greater Atlanta	**(404) 527-7630**
Augusta, CCCS/Central Savannah River Area	**(706) 736-2090**
Calhoun, Family and Children's Services	1-800-459-2227
Carrollton, CCCS of Greater Atlanta	1-800-251-2227
Columbus, CCCS	**(706) 327-3239**
Covington, CCCS of Greater Atlanta	(404) 527-7630
Dalton, Family and Children's Services	1-800-459-2227
Decatur, CCCS of Greater Atlanta	(404) 527-7630
Douglasville, CCCS of Greater Atlanta	(404) 527-7630
Fayetteville, CCCS of Greater Atlanta	(404) 527-7630
Gainesville, CCCS of Greater Atlanta	1-800-251-2227
Kings Bay NAS, CCCS of Jacksonville	(904) 396-4846
Lagrange, CCCS	(706) 845-7204
Macon, CCCS of Middle Georgia	**(912) 745-6197**
Marietta, CCCS of Greater Atlanta	(404) 527-7630
Millegeville, CCCS of Middle Georgia	1-800-446-7123
Norcross, CCCS of Greater Atlanta	(404) 527-7630
Rome, CCCS of Greater Atlanta	1-800-251-2227
Savannah, CCCS/Savannah Area	**(912) 927-4357**
Thomasville, CCCS of Central FL	(904) 878-0975
Thomson, CCCS/Central Savannah River Area	1-800-736-0033
Tifton, CCCS of Southwest Georgia	(912) 883-0909
Toccoa, CCCS of Greater Atlanta	1-800-251-2227
Valdosta, CCCS of Southwest Georgia	(912) 883-0909
Warner Robins, CCCS of Middle Georgia	1-800-446-7123
Waycross, CCCS of Jacksonville	(912) 284-2261
Waynesboro, CCCS/Central Savannah River Area	1-800-736-0033
West Point, CCCS	(706) 845-7204

HAWAII

Hilo, CCCS of Hawaii	1-800-801-5999

Honolulu, CCCS of Hawaii	(808) 973-7133
Honolulu, Hawaii Credit Counseling	(808) 842-5777
Wailuku, CCCS of Hawaii	1-800-801-5999

IDAHO

Boise, CCCS of Idaho	(208) 375-8140
Coeur d'Alene, CCCS/Inland Northwest	1-800-892-6854
Lewiston, CCCS of Northern Idaho	(208) 746-0127
Moscow, CCCS of Northern Idaho	1-800-556-0127
Nampa, CCCS of Idaho	(208) 375-8140
Sandpoint, CCCS/Inland Northwest	1-800-892-6854

ILLINOIS

Algonquin, CCCS of McHenry County	(815) 338-5757
Alton, Chestnut Credit Counseling	1-800-615-3022
Alton, CCCS of St. Louis	1-800-966-3328
Aurora, CCCS of Aurora	(630) 844-3327
Carpentersville, CCCS of Elgin	(847) 931-1260
Champaign, CCCS East Central Illinois	1-800-959-2227
Chicago, Metro Family Service/CCCS	1-888-239-2227
Chicago, CCCS of Greater Chicago	(312) 849-2227
Chicago Heights, CCCS of Greater Chicago	1-888-527-3328
Chicago/SW, CCCS of Greater Chicago	(773) 233-2232
Collinsville, Chestnut Credit Counseling	1-800-615-3022
Crystal Lake, CCCS of McHenry County	(815) 338-5757
Danville, CCCS East Central Illinois	1-800-959-2227
Decatur, Chestnut Credit Counseling	1-800-615-3022
Decatur, CCCS East Central Illinois	(217) 425-0654
Edwardsville, Chestnut Credit Counseling	1-800-615-3022
Effingham, CCCS of St. Louis	1-800-966-3328
Elgin, CCCS of Elgin	(847) 931-1260
Fairview Heights, CCCS of St. Louis	1-800-966-3328
Farmington, CCCS of St. Louis	1-800-966-3328
Granite City, Chestnut Credit Counseling	1-800-615-3022
Highland Park, CCCS of Catholic Charities	(847) 249-0000

Hoffman Estates, CCCS of Elgin	(847) 931-1260
Joliet, CCCS of Joliet	**(815) 741-0848**
Libertyville, CCCS of Catholic Charities	(847) 249-0000
Lisle, CCCS of Greater Chicago	(630) 512-0077
Marion, CCCS of St. Louis	1-800-966-3328
Matteson, CCCS of Greater Chicago	1-888-527-3328
Mattoon, CCCS of St. Louis	1-800-966-3328
Moline, CCCS of Northwest Illinois	1-800-547-5005
Mt. Carmel, CCCS of Tri-State	1-800-451-6293
Mt. Vernon, CCCS of St. Louis	1-800-966-3328
Naperville, Metro Family Service/CCCS	1-888-239-2227
Normal, CCCS of North Central Illinois	**(309) 451-8300**
Oak Park, CCCS of Greater Chicago	(708) 445-2190
Olney, CCCS of Tri-State	1-800-451-6293
Orland Park, Metro Family Service/CCCS	1-888-239-2227
Pekin, Chestnut Credit Counseling	1-800-615-3022
Peoria, Chestnut Credit Counseling	1-800-615-3022
Peoria, CCCS of Central Illinois	**(309) 676-2941**
Quincy, CCCS of St. Louis	1-800-966-3328
Rockford, CCCS of Greater Chicago	(815) 964-9333
Rolling Meadows, Metro Family Service/CCCS	**1-888-239-2227**
Round Lake, CCCS of Catholic Charities	(847) 249-0000
Schaumburg, CCCS of Greater Chicago	(847) 995-1343
Skokie, Metro Family Service/CCCS	1-888-239-2227
Springfield, CCCS of St. Louis	1-800-966-3328
St. Charles, CCCS of Aurora	(630) 844-3327
Streamwood, CCCS of Elgin, (847) 931-1260	
Sugar Grove, CCCS of Aurora	(630) 844-3327
Tinley Park, CCCS of Greater Chicago	(708) 614-0440
Waukegan, CCCS of Catholic Charities	**(847) 249-0000**
Wheaton, Metro Family Service/CCCS	1-888-239-2227
Wheeling, CCCS of Greater Chicago	(847) 537-5808
Woodstock, CCCS of McHenry County	**(815) 338-5757**

INDIANA

Anderson, CCCS of Central Indiana	(765) 266-1300
Bedford, CCCS of Central Indiana	(812) 849-4457

Bloomington, CCCS of Central Indiana	(317) 266-1300
Chesterton, CCCS of Northwest Indiana	1-800-982-4801
Columbus, CCCS of Central Indiana	(317) 266-1300
Connersville, CCCS of Central Indiana	(765) 827-0553
Crawfordsville, CCCS of Central Indiana	(765) 362-4096
Elkhart, CCCS of Northern Indiana	**(219) 293-0075**
Evansville, CCCS of Tri-State	**(812) 422-1108**
Ft. Wayne, CCCS of Northeastern Indiana	**1-800-432-0420**
Gary, CCCS of Northwest Indiana	**(219) 980-4800**
Greensburg, CCCS of Central Indiana	(317) 266-1300
Griffith, CCCS of Northwest Indiana	(219) 980-4800
Hammond, CCCS of Northwest Indiana	1-800-982-4801
Indianapolis, CCCS of Central Indiana	**(317) 266-1300**
Kendallville, CCCS of Northeastern Indiana	1-800-432-0420
Kokomo, CCCS of North Central Indiana	**(765) 454-7290**
Lafayette, CCCS of Lafayette	**1-800-875-5361**
Laporte, CCCS of Northwest Indiana	1-800-982-4801
Lawrenceburg, CCCS of Greater Cincinnati	(513) 651-0111
Marion, CCCS of Central Indiana	(317) 266-1300
Merrillville, CCCS of Northwest Indiana	(219) 980-4800
Michigan City, CCCS of Northwest Indiana	1-800-982-4801
Middlebury, CCCS of Northern Indiana	1-800-794-6559
Muncie, CCCS of Central Indiana	(317) 266-1300
New Castle, CCCS of Central Indiana	(317) 266-1300
Portage, CCCS of Northwest Indiana	1-800-982-4801
Rensselaer, CCCS of Northwest Indiana	1-800-982-4801
Richmond, CCCS of the Miami Valley	1-800-377-2432
Seymour, CCCS of Central Indiana	(317) 266-1300
South Bend, CCCS of Northern Indiana	1-800-794-6559
Terre Haute, CCCS of Central Indiana	(317) 266-1300
Valparaiso, CCCS of Northwest Indiana	1-800-982-4801
Vincennes, CCCS of Tri-State	1-800-451-6293
Warsaw, CCCS of Northeastern Indiana	1-800-432-0420

IOWA

Ames, CCCS of Des Moines	(515) 287-6428
Bettendorf, CCCS of Des Moines	1-800-838-8830

Burlington, CCCS/Family Service Agency	1-800-826-3574
Cedar Rapids, CCCS/Family Service Agency	**(319) 398-3574**
Des Moines, CCCS of Des Moines	**(515) 287-6428**
Mason City, CCCS of Northeastern IA	(515) 421-7619
Sioux City, CCCS of Greater Siouxland	**1-800-509-5601**
Spencer, CCCS of Greater Siouxland	1-800-509-5601
Waterloo, CCCS of Northeastern IA	**(319) 234-0661**

KANSAS

Emporia, CCCS of Topeka	(316) 342-7788
Garden City, CCCS	1-800-279-2227
Hays, CCCS	1-800-279-2227
Hutchinson, CCCS	1-800-279-2227
Kansas City, CCCS/Greater Kansas City	(816) 753-0535
Lawrence, CCCS of Topeka	(785) 749-4224
Leavenworth, CCCS/Greater Kansas City	(816) 753-0535
Manhatten, CCCS of Topeka	(785) 539-6666
Overland Park, CCCS/Greater Kansas City	(816) 753-0535
Pittsburg, CCCS of Springfield	1-800-346-4930
Salina, CCCS	**(785) 827-6731**
Topeka, CCCS of Topeka	**(785) 234-0217**
Wichita, CCCS	(316) 265-2000

KENTUCKY

Ashland, CCCS of Family Service	(304) 522-4321
Bowling Green, CCCS of Central Ohio	(502) 781-5989
Corbin, CCCS of East Tennessee	1-800-358-9231
Covington, CCCS of Greater Cincinnati	(513) 651-0111
Elizabethtown, CCCS of Central Ohio	(502) 769-0101
Florence, CCCS of Greater Cincinnati	(513) 651-0111
Fort Campbell, CCCS of St. Louis	1-800-966-3328
Frankfort, CCCS of Central Ohio	(502) 223-5604
Lexington, CCCS of Central Ohio	(606) 272-8028
Louisville, CCCS of Louisville	**(502) 561-3716**
Louisville, Trademark Credit Counseling	(502) 458-8840

Madisonville, CCCS of Tri-State	1-800-451-6293
Mayfield, CCCS of St. Louis	1-800-966-3328
Owensboro, CCCS of Tri-State	1-800-451-6293
Paducah, CCCS of St. Louis	1-800-966-3328
Pikeville, CCCS of Central Ohio	(606) 432-5337

LOUISIANA

Alexandria, Budget Management Services	**(318) 448-9783**
Alexandria, CCCS	(318) 448-9783
Baton Rouge, CCCS	**(504) 927-4274**
Baton Rouge, CCCS	(504) 927-4274
Bossier City, CCCS	(318) 861-4693
Covington, CCCS/Greater New Orleans	(504) 893-0650
Gonzales, CCCS	(504) 647-4259
Gretna, CCCS/Greater New Orleans	(504) 366-8952
Hammond, CCCS	(504) 543-0396
Houma, CCCS/Greater New Orleans	(504) 876-2225
Kenner, CCCS/Greater New Orleans	(504) 443-1015
Lafayette, CCCS	(318) 232-4693
Lake Charles, CCCS	(318) 477-4693
Leesville, Budget Management Services	(318) 448-9783
Monroe, CCCS	(318) 322-3645
Morgan City, CCCS/Greater New Orleans	(504) 385-2055
Natchitoches, CCCS	(318) 357-8382
New Iberia, CCCS	(318) 367-5895
New Orleans, CCCS/Greater New Orleans	**(504) 529-2396**
Opelousas, CCCS	1-800-850-2227
Ruston, CCCS	(318) 255-0410
Shreveport, CCCS	(318) 861-4693
Slidell, CCCS/Greater New Orleans	(504) 641-4158
Zachary, CCCS	(504) 927-4274

MAINE

Auburn, CCCS of Maine	1-800-539-2227
Augusta, CCCS of Maine	1-800-539-2227

Bangor, CCCS of Maine	1-800-539-2227
Bath, CCCS of Maine	1-800-539-2227
Brunswick/NAS, CCCS of Maine	1-800-539-2227
Farmington, CCCS of Maine	1-800-539-2227
Ogunquit, CCCS of Maine	1-800-539-2227
Portland, CCCS of Maine	**(207) 773-1411**
Presque Isle, CCCS of Maine	1-800-539-2227
Rockland, CCCS of Maine	1-800-539-2227
Saco, CCCS of Maine	1-800-539-2227
Sanford, CCCS of Maine	1-800-539-2227

MARYLAND

Annapolis, CCCS of Southeast MD	(410) 573-9090
Bel Air, CCCS of MD & DE	1-800-642-2227
Brooklyn Park, CCCS of MD & DE	(410) 747-6803
Catonsville, CCCS of MD & DE	**(410) 747-6803**
Columbia, CCCS of MD & DE	(410) 747-6803
Dundalk, CCCS of MD & DE	(410) 747-6803
Easton, CCCS of MD & DE	1-800-642-2227
Frederick, CCCS/Greater Washington	1-800-747-4222
Hagerstown, CCCS/Greater Washington	1-800-747-4222
Lanham, CCCS of Southeast MD	(301) 459-8766
Laurel, CCCS of MD & DE	**1-800-642-2227**
Lexington Park, CCCS of Southeast MD	(301) 862-5552
Owings Mills, CCCS of MD & DE	(410) 747-6803
Oxon Hill, CCCS of Southeast MD	(301) 839-8794
Perry Hall, CCCS of MD & DE	(410) 747-6803
Rockville, CCCS/Greater Washington	**1-800-747-4222**
Salisbury, CCCS of MD & DE	1-800-642-2227
Severna Park, CCCS of Southeast MD	(410) 544-9666
Silver Spring, CCCS/Greater Washington	1-800-747-4222
Upper Marlboro, CCCS of Southeast MD	(301) 952-9204
Waldorf, CCCS of Southeast MD	(301) 705-9880

MASSACHUSETTS

Amherst, CCCS of Massachusetts	1-800-282-6196

Beverly, CCCS of Massachusetts	1-800-282-6196
Boston, CCCS of Massachusetts	**1-800-282-6196**
Brockton, CCCS of Massachusetts	1-800-282-6196
Fall River, CCCS of Massachusetts	1-800-282-6196
Falmouth, CCCS of Massachusetts	1-800-282-6196
Fitchburg, CCCS of Massachusetts	1-800-282-6196
Framingham, CCCS of Massachusetts	1-800-282-6196
Great Barrington, CCCS of Massachusetts	1-800-282-6196
Hyannis, CCCS of Massachusetts	1-800-282-6196
Lowell, CCCS of Massachusetts	1-800-282-6196
New Bedford, CCCS of Massachusetts	1-800-282-6196
North Adams, CCCS of Massachusetts	1-800-282-6196
Orleans, CCCS of Massachusetts	1-800-282-6196
Pittsfield, CCCS of Massachusetts	1-800-282-6196
Quincy, CCCS of Massachusetts	1-800-282-6196
Springfield, CCCS of Massachusetts	1-800-282-6196
Waltham, CCCS of Massachusetts	1-800-282-6196
Woburn, CCCS of Massachusetts	1-800-282-6196
Worcester, CCCS of Massachusetts	1-800-282-6196

MICHIGAN

Allen Park, CCCS of Michigan	1-800-547-5005
Ann Arbor, CCCS of Michigan	1-800-547-5005
Auburn Hills, CCCS of Michigan	1-800-547-5005
Battle Creek, CCCS of Michigan	1-800-547-5005
Benton Harbor, CCCS of Michigan	1-800-547-5005
Brighton, CCCS of Michigan	1-800-547-5005
Detroit, CCCS of Michigan	1-800-547-5005
East Lansing, CCCS of Michigan	1-800-547-5005
Eastpointe, CCCS of Michigan	1-800-547-5005
Farmington Hills, CCCS of Michigan	**1-800-547-5005**
Flint, CCCS of Michigan	1-800-547-5005
Gaylord, CCCS of Michigan	1-800-547-5005
Grand Rapids, CCCS of Michigan	1-800-547-5005
Holland, CCCS of Michigan	1-800-547-5005
Iron Mountain, CCCS of Michigan	1-800-547-5005

Jackson, CCCS of Michigan	1-800-547-5005
Kentwood, CCCS of Michigan	1-800-547-5005
Lansing, CCCS of Michigan	1-800-547-5005
Marquette, CCCS of Michigan	1-800-547-5005
Monroe, CCCS of Michigan	1-800-547-5005
Mount Clemens, CCCS of Michigan	1-800-547-5005
Muskegon, CCCS of Michigan	1-800-547-5005
Novi, CCCS of Michigan	1-800-547-5005
Port Huron, CCCS of Michigan	1-800-547-5005
Portage, CCCS of Michigan	1-800-547-5005
Saginaw, CCCS of Michigan	1-800-547-5005
Southfield, CCCS of Michigan	1-800-547-5005
Traverse City, CCCS of Michigan	1-800-547-5005
Troy, CCCS of Michigan	1-800-547-5005
Westland, CCCS of Michigan	1-800-547-5005

MINNESOTA

Apple Valley, CCCS of Minnesota	(612) 349-6953
Austin, CCCS of Rochester	(507) 281-6299
Bemidji, CCCS of Duluth	1-800-777-7419
Blaine, LSS Financial Counseling Service	(612) 774-9507
Brainerd, Village Family Service Center	1-800-450-4019
Cambridge, CCCS of Duluth	1-800-777-7419
Cloquet, CCCS of Duluth	(218) 726-4767
Coon Rapids, CCCS of Minnesota	(612) 349-6953
Crystal, Village Financial Counseling Service	1-800-450-4019
Duluth, CCCS of Duluth	**(218) 726-4767**
Faribault, CCCS of Duluth	(507) 625-8021
Forest Lake, CCCS/Family Service St. Croix	1-800-780-2890
Grand Rapids, CCCS of Duluth	(218) 326-1269
Hibbing, CCCS of Duluth	(218) 263-5433
Little Canada, CCCS of Minnesota	(612) 349-6953
Mankato, CCCS of Duluth	(507) 625-8021
Maplewood, Family Service	(612) 222-0311
Marshall, CCCS of Duluth	(507) 537-0030
Minneapolis, CCCS of Minnesota	**(612) 349-6953**

Minnetonka, CCCS of Minnesota	(612) 349-6953
Morehead, Village Family Service Center	1-800-450-4019
Mora, CCCS of Duluth	1-800-777-7419
New Ulm, CCCS of Duluth	(507) 625-8021
Owatonna, Credit Counseling of Owatonna	(507) 281-6299
Red Wing, CCCS of Duluth	1-800-777-7419
Redwood Falls, CCCS of Duluth	(320) 235-7916
Rochester, CCCS of Rochester	**(507) 281-6299**
St. Paul, CCCS of Minnesota	(612) 349-6953
Saint Paul, Family Service	**(612) 222-0311**
St. Paul, LSS Financial Couseling Service	(612) 774-9507
Saint Paul/South, Family Service	(612) 222-0311
St. Cloud, Village Family Service Center	1-800-450-4019
Stillwater, CCCS Family Service St. Croix	**(612) 439-4840**
Willmar, CCCS of Duluth	(320) 235-7916
Woodbury, CCCS Family Service St. Croix	(612) 735-5405

MISSISSIPPI

Biloxi, CCCS/Greater New Orleans	(601) 435-2227
Hattiesburg, CCCS/Greater New Orleans	(601) 435-2227
Jackson, CCCS/Greater New Orleans	(601) 362-3223
Jackson, CCCS of Jackson	**(601) 352-7784**
Meridian, CCCS/Greater New Orleans	(601) 485-7722
Pascagoula, CCCS/Greater New Orleans	(601) 762-9988
Southaven, Family Service of Memphis-CCCS	(901) 323-4909
Tupelo, CCCS/Greater New Orleans	(601) 680-9750
Vicksburg, CCCS of Jackson	(601) 352-7784

MISSOURI

Arnold, CCCS of St. Louis	(314) 647-9004
Belton, CCCS/Greater Kansas City	(816) 753-0535
Branson, CCCS of Springfield	1-800-882-0808
Camdenton, CCCS of Mid-Missouri	(573) 443-0303
Cape Girardeau, CCCS of St. Louis	1-800-966-3328
Columbia, CCCS of Mid-Missouri	**(573) 443-0303**

Farmington, CCCS of St. Louis	1-800-966-3328
Ft. Leonard Wood, CCCS of Mid-Missouri	(573) 443-0303
Hannibal, CCCS of St. Louis	1-800-966-3328
Independence, CCCS/Greater Kansas City	(816) 753-0535
Jefferson City, CCCS of Mid-Missouri	1-800-243-7722
Joplin, CCCS of Springfield	(417) 782-6830
Kansas City, CCCS/Greater Kansas City	**(816) 753-0535**
Kansas City, CCCS/Greater Kansas City	(816) 753-0535
Kansas City/N, CCCS/Greater Kansas City	(816) 753-0535
Kansas City/S, CCCS/Greater Kansas City	(816) 753-0535
N. St. Louis County, CCCS of St. Louis	(314) 647-9004
Poplar Bluff, CCCS of St. Louis	1-800-966-3328
Sedalia, CCCS/Greater Kansas City	(816) 753-0535
Springfield, CCCS of Springfield	**(417) 889-7474**
St. Charles, CCCS of St. Louis	(314) 647-9004
St. Joseph, CCCS/Greater Kansas City	(816) 753-0535
St. Louis, CCCS of St. Louis	**(314) 647-9004**
Warrensburg, CCCS/Greater Kansas City	(816) 753-0535
West Plains, CCCS of Springfield	(417) 256-4082

MONTANA

Billings, CCCS of Billings	**1-800-227-7539**
Bozeman, CCCS of Billings	(406) 582-9273
Bozeman, Credit Education & Budgeting Service	1-800-901-9273
Butte, CCCS of Cascade County	(406) 723-5176
Great Falls, CCCS of Cascade County	**(406) 761-8721**
Havre, CCCS of Cascade County	(406) 265-3633
Helena, CCCS of Cascade County	(406) 443-1774
Kalispell, CCCS of Cascade County	(406) 257-4069
Lewistown, CCCS of Cascade County	(406) 761-8721
Miles City, CCCS of Billings	1-800-227-7539
Missoula, CCCS of Cascade County	(406) 543-1188

NEBRASKA

| Grand Island, CCCS of Nebraska | (308) 381-4551 |
| Lincoln, CCCS of Nebraska | (402) 484-7200 |

Norfolk, CCCS of Nebraska   (402) 371-4656
North Platte, CCCS of Nebraska   (308) 532-9760
Omaha, CCCS of Nebraska   **(402) 333-2227**
Scottsbluff, CCCS of Nebraska   1-800-808-2227

NEVADA

Elko, CCCS of Northern Nevada   (702) 753-4966
Henderson, CCCS of Southern Nevada   (702) 364-0344
Las Vegas, CCCS of Southern Nevada   **(702) 364-0344**
Laughlin, CCCS of Southern Nevada   1-800-451-4505
Nellis AFB, CCCS of Southern Nevada   (702) 364-0344
North Las Vegas, CCCS of Southern Nevada   (702) 364-0344
Reno, CCCS of Northern Nevada   **(702) 322-6557**

NEW HAMPSHIRE

Berlin, CCCS of NH & VT   1-800-327-6778
Colebrook, CCCS of NH & VT   1-800-327-6778
Concord, CCCS of NH & VT   **1-800-660-5609**
Dover, CCCS of NH & VT   1-800-327-6778
Keene, CCCS of NH & VT   1-800-327-6778
Laconia, CCCS of NH & VT   1-800-327-6778
Lebanon, CCCS of NH & VT   1-800-327-6778
Littleton, CCCS of NH & VT   1-800-327-6778
Manchester, CCCS of NH & VT   1-800-327-6778
Nashua, CCCS of NH & VT   1-800-327-6778
Petersborough, CCCS of NH & VT   1-800-327-6778
Tilton, CCCS of NH & VT   1-800-327-6778

NEW JERSEY

Absecon Highlands, CCCS of South Jersey   **1-800-473-2227**
Atlantic City, CCCS of South Jersey   1-800-473-2227
Cape May Courthouse, CCCS of South Jersey   1-800-473-2227
Cedar Knolls, CCCS of New Jersey   **(973) 267-4324**
Cherry Hill, CCCS/Delaware Valley   (215) 563-5665
Egg Harbor Township, CCCS of South Jersey   1-800-473-2227

Flemington, CCCS of Central New Jersey	(908) 788-7710
Franklin, CCCS of New Jersey	(973) 267-4324
Freehold, Family & Children's Service	(732) 531-7272
Hammonton, CCCS of South Jersey	1-800-473-2227
Hasbrouck Heights, CCCS of New Jersey	(973) 267-4324
Mahwah, CCCS of New Jersey	(973) 267-4324
Manahawkin, CCCS of South Jersey	1-800-473-2227
Montclair, CCCS of New Jersey	(973) 267-4324
Mt. Holly, CCCS of Central New Jersey	(609) 265-2424
New Brunswick, CCCS of New Jersey	(973) 267-4324
Oakhurst, Family & Children's Service	**(908) 531-7272**
Plainfield, CCCS of New Jersey	(973) 267-4324
Plainsboro, CCCS of Central New Jersey	(609) 585-8220
Pleasantville, CCCS of South Jersey	1-800-473-2227
Princeton, CCCS of Central New Jersey	(609) 924-1320
Ridgewood, CCCS of New Jersey	(973) 267-4324
Somerville, CCCS of New Jersey	(973) 267-4324
Toms River, Family & Children's Service	(732) 531-7272
Trenton, CCCS of Central New Jersey	**(609) 585-8220**
Turnersville, CCCS of South Jersey	1-800-473-2227
Vineland, CCCS of South Jersey	1-800-473-2227
Woodbury, CCCS of South Jersey	1-800-473-2227

NEW MEXICO

Albuquerque, CCCS Southwest	(505) 884-6601
Albuquerque, CCCS Southwest	(505) 839-9402
Clovis, CCCS of Greater Dallas	(505) 763-2227
Farmington, CCCS Southwest	(505) 325-5631
Hobbs, CCCS of Greater Fort Worth	(505) 397-7786
Las Cruces, CCCS Southwest	(505) 527-2585
Roswell, CCCS Southwest	1-800-308-2227
Santa Fe, CCCS Southwest	1-800-308-2227

NEW YORK

Albany, CCCS/Central New York	(518) 482-2227

Amherst, CCCS of Buffalo	1-800-926-9685
Binghamton, CCCS/Central New York	(607) 770-9657
Brooklyn, CCCS/Southern New York	1-800-547-5005
Buffalo, CCCS of Buffalo	**1-800-926-9685**
Hicksville, CCCS/Southern New York	1-800-547-5005
Manhattan, CCCS/Southern New York	1-800-547-5005
Queens, CCCS/Southern New York	(718) 275-9800
Rochester, CCCS of Rochester	**(716) 546-3440**
Staten Island, CCCS/Southern New York	1-800-547-5005
Syracuse, CCCS/Central New York	**1-800-479-6026**
Utica, CCCS/Central New York	(315) 797-5366
White Plains, CCCS/Southern New York	1-800-547-5005
Yonkers, CCCS/Southern New York	1-800-547-5005

NORTH CAROLINA

Asheville, CCCS/Western NC	**1-800-737-5485**
Burlington, CCCS of Burlington	(910) 226-4175
Canton, CCCS/Western NC	1-800-737-5485
Cary, CCCS	(919) 821-1770
Chapel Hill, CCCS	(919) 933-4226
Chapel Hill, Community Financial Counseling	(919) 932-3115
Charlotte, CCCS	**(704) 332-4191**
Concord, CCCS	(704) 786-7918
Dover, CCCS/Western NC	1-800-737-5485
Durham, CCCS of Durham	**(919) 688-3381**
Elizabeth City, CCCS of Virginia	(919) 335-9160
Fayetteville, CCCS of Fayetteville	**(919) 323-3192**
Franklin, CCCS/Western NC	1-800-737-5485
Gastonia, CCCS of Gaston County	**(704) 864-7704**
Goldsboro, CCCS of Fayetteville	(919) 580-1060
Greensboro, CCCS of Greater Greensboro	**(910) 373-8882**
Greenville, CCCS of Virginia	(919) 335-1156
Henderson, CCCS of Durham	(919) 688-3381
Hendersonville, CCCS/Western NC	1-800-737-5485
Hendersonville, CCCS/Western NC	1-800-737-5485

Hickory, CCCS of Hickory	**(704) 322-7161**
High Point, CCCS of High Point	**(910) 889-6108**
Jacksonville, CCCS Family Services	(910) 799-8734
Lexington, CCCS of Forsyth County	(704) 249-0237
Lincolnton, CCCS of Gaston County	(704) 735-0908
Monroe, CCCS	(704) 226-5120
Morganton, CCCS of Hickory	(704) 438-3880
Oxford, CCCS of Durham	(919) 688-3381
Pisgah Forest, CCCS/Western NC	1-800-737-5485
Raleigh, CCCS	**(919) 821-1770**
Rocky Mount, CCCS of Virginia	(919) 977-2227
Salisbury, CCCS of Virginia	(704) 636-0089
Shelby, CCCS of Gaston County	(704) 481-9419
Spindale, CCCS of Spindale	**(704) 286-7062**
Sylva, CCCS/Western NC	1-800-737-5485
Wentworth, CCCS of Greater Greensboro	(910) 342-8247
Wilmington, CCCS Family Services	**(910) 799-8734**
Winston-Salem, CCCS of Forsyth County	**(910) 725-1958**
Yadkinville, CCCS of Forsyth County	(910) 679-4462

NORTH DAKOTA

Bismarck, Village Family Service	1-800-450-4019
Fargo, Village Family Service	**(701) 235-3328**
Grand Forks, Village Family Service	1-800-450-4019
Jamestown, Village Family Service	1-800-450-4019
Minot, Village Family Service	1-800-450-4019

OHIO

Akron, CCCS of Akron	**(330) 376-4151**
Alliance, CCCS of Stark County	1-800-355-2227
Astabula, CCCS of Astabula	**(216) 992-0300**
Athens, CCCS of the Mid-Ohio Valley	1-800-882-4924
Batavia, CCCS of Greater Cincinnati	(513) 651-0111
Bellefontaine, CCCS	(513) 592-2227

Bowling Green, CCCS of Central Ohio	(419) 531-2227
Brunswick, CCCS/Northeastern OH	(216) 781-8624
Canton, CCCS of Stark County	**1-800-355-2227**
Chillicothe, CCCS of Central Ohio	(614) 621-4293
Cincinnati, CCCS of Greater Cincinnati	**(513) 651-0111**
Cleveland, CCCS/Northeastern OH	**(216) 781-8624**
Cleveland Heights, CCCS/Northeastern OH	(216) 781-8624
Columbus, CCCS of Central Ohio	**(614) 621-4293**
Dayton, CCCS of the Miami Valley	**1-800-377-2432**
Defiance, CCCS of Central Ohio	(419) 531-2227
Dalaware, CCCS of Central Ohio	(614) 621-4293
Dover, CCCS of Stark County	1-800-355-2227
East Liverpool, CCCS of Columbiana County	(216) 386-3328
Fairfield, CCCS of Butler County	(513) 868-9220
Findlay, CCCS	(419) 425-5320
Flushing, CCCS/Upper Ohio Valley	1-800-220-3252
Hamilton, CCCS of Butler County	**(513) 868-9220**
Kent, CCCS of Portage County	**(330) 678-3911**
Kenton, CCCS	(419) 675-7210
Lancaster, CCCS of Central Ohio	(614) 621-4293
Lima, CCCS	**(419) 227-9202**
Lisbon, CCCS of Columbiana County	**(330) 424-7991**
Lisbon, Community Action Credit Counseling	**(330) 424-4013**
Lorain, CCCS/Northeastern OH	(216) 781-8624
Mansfield, CCCS of Central Ohio	(614) 621-4293
Marion, CCCS of Central Ohio	(614) 621-4293
Marysville, CCCS of Central Ohio	(614) 621-4293
Mason, CCCS of Butler County	(513) 573-9429
Mentor, CCCS/Northeastern OH	(216) 781-8624
Middletown, CCCS of Butler County	(513) 424-6888
Mt. Vernon, CCCS Family Counseling Service	1-800-686-2756
Newark, CCCS Family Counseling Service	**1-800-686-2756**
Norwood, CCCS of Greater Cincinnati	(513) 651-0111
Oxford, CCCS of Butler County	(513) 868-9220
Parma, CCCS/Northeastern OH	(216) 781-8624
Portsmouth, CCCS of Family Service	(304) 522-4321
Salem, CCCS of Columbiana County	(330) 332-9900

Sandusky, CCCS of Central Ohio	(419) 531-2227
Sidney, CCCS of the Miami Valley	1-800-377-2432
Springfield, CCCS of the Miami Valley	1-800-377-2432
Steubenville, CCCS/Upper Ohio Valley	1-800-220-3252
Toledo, CCCS of Central Ohio	(419) 531-2227
Van Wert, CCCS	(419) 238-0677
Warren, CCCS of Warren	**(330) 856-2907**
Wash. Courthouse, CCCS of Butler County	(614) 335-7282
West Chester, CCCS of Butler County	(513) 868-9220
Wooster, CCCS of Stark County	1-800-355-2227
Youngstown, CCCS of Youngstown	**(330) 782-9113**

OKLAHOMA

Ada, CCCS of Central Oklahoma	1-800-364-2227
Altus, CCCS of Central Oklahoma	1-800-364-2227
Ardmore, CCCS of Greater Dallas	1-800-364-2227
Bartlesville, CCCS of Oklahoma	(918) 336-7619
Bethany, CCCS of Central Oklahoma	**(405) 789-2227**
Broken Arrow, CCCS of Oklahoma	(918) 744-5611
Chickasha, CCCS of Central Oklahoma	1-800-364-2227
Claremont, CCCS of Oklahoma	(918) 434-3133
Del City, CCCS of Central Oklahoma	(405) 677-8111
Duncan, CCCS of Central Oklahoma	1-800-364-2227
Durant, CCCS of Durant	1-800-364-2227
Edmond, CCCS of Central Oklahoma	(405) 341-4443
Enid, CCCS of Central Oklahoma	(405) 233-2227
Guthrie, CCCS of Central Oklahoma	1-800-364-2227
Lawton, CCCS of Central Oklahoma	(405) 357-3932
McAlester, CCCS of Oklahoma	1-800-324-5611
Muskogee, CCCS of Oklahoma	(918) 744-5611
Norman, CCCS of Central Oklahoma	(405) 360-9916
Oklahoma City, CCCS of Central Oklahoma	(405) 691-6801
Okmulgee, CCCS of Oklahoma	(918) 744-5611
Owasso, CCCS of Oklahoma	(918) 744-5611
Ponca City, CCCS of Central Oklahoma	1-800-364-2227

Sapulpa, CCCS of Oklahoma	(918) 744-5611
Shawnee, CCCS of Central Oklahoma	(405) 360-9916
Stillwater, CCCS of Central Oklahoma	1-800-364-2227
Tinker AFB, CCCS of Central Oklahoma	(405) 739-2747
Tulsa, CCCS of Oklahoma	**(918) 744-5611**
Tulsa, CCCS of Oklahoma	(918) 744-5611
Watonga, CCCS of Central Oklahoma	1-800-364-2227
Weatherford, CCCS of Central Oklahoma	1-800-364-2227

OREGON

Albany, CCCS of Linn-Benton	**(541) 926-5843**
Astoria, CCCS of Oregon	(503) 325-4877
Beaverton, CCCS of Oregon	(503) 232-8139
Bend, CCCS of Central Oregon	**1-800-285-4605**
Coos Bay, CCCS of Coos-Curry	**(541) 888-7040**
Corvallis, CCCS of Linn-Benton	(541) 926-5843
Eugene, CCCS of Lane County	**(541) 342-4459**
Florence, CCCS of Lane County	(503) 997-8990
Gold Beach, CCCS of Coos-Curry	1-800-248-7040
Grants Pass, CCCS of Grant's Pass	**(541) 479-6002**
Gresham, CCCS of Oregon	(503) 232-8139
Hillsboro, CCCS of Oregon	(503) 232-8139
Klamath Falls, CCCS/Southern Oregon	(541) 883-8118
Lapine, CCCS of Central Oregon	1-800-285-4605
Madras, CCCS of Central Oregon	1-800-285-4605
McMinnville, CCCS of Oregon	(503) 434-2882
Medford, CCCS/Southern Oregon	**(541) 779-2273**
Oregon City, CCCS of Oregon	(503) 232-8139
Pendleton, CCCS of Umatilla County	**(541) 276-3856**
Portland, CCCS of Oregon	**(503) 232-8139**
Prineville, CCCS of Central Oregon	1-800-285-4605
Roseburg, Douglas CCCS	**(541) 673-3104**
Salem, CCCS/Mid-Williamette Valley	**(503) 581-7301**
Salem, Credit Counselor's of Salem	(503) 581-3058
Springfield, CCCS of Lane County	(541) 342-4459
The Dalles, CCCS of Oregon	(541) 296-4445
Wilsonville, CCCS of Oregon	(503) 232-8139

PENNSYLVANIA

Beaver, CCCS of Western PA	(412) 744-0798
Bloomsburg, CCCS of Northeastern PA	1-800-922-9537
Butler, CCCS of Western PA	(412) 282-7812
Carlisle, CCCS of Carlisle	(717) 541-1757
Coatesville, CCCS of Central PA	(215) 383-4535
Duncansville, CCCS of Western PA	(814) 696-3546
Easton, CCCS of Lehigh Valley	(610) 821-4010
Erie, CCCS of Northwestern PA	**(814) 864-0605**
Greencastle, CCCS of Central PA	(717) 397-5182
Greensburg, CCCS of Western PA	(412) 282-7812
Harrisburg, CCCS/Greater Harrisburg	(717) 541-1757
Hazleton, CCCS of Northeastern PA	1-800-922-9537
Honesdale, CCCS of Northeastern PA	1-800-922-9537
Jim Thorpe, CCCS of Lehigh Valley	1-800-220-2733
Johnstown, CCCS of Western PA	(814) 539-6335
Lancaster, CCCS of Central PA	**(717) 397-5183**
Lebanon, CCCS of Central PA	(717) 397-5182
Meadville, CCCS of Northwestern PA	(814) 337-4455
Meadville, CCCS of Western PA	(814) 333-8570
Milford, CCCS of Northeastern PA	1-800-922-9537
New Castle, CCCS of Western PA	(412) 652-8074
New Hope, CCCS of Lehigh Valley	1-800-220-2733
Norristown, CCCS/Delaware Valley	(215) 563-5665
Pen Argyl, CCCS of Lehigh Valley	(610) 821-4010
Philadelphia, CCCS/Delaware Valley	**1-800-989-2227**
Pittsburgh, CCCS of Western PA	**(412) 471-7584**
Pottstown, CCCS of Lehigh Valley	1-800-220-2733
Pottsville, CCCS of Lehigh Valley	1-800-220-2733
Quakertown, CCCS of Lehigh Valley	1-800-220-2733
Reading, CCCS of Lehigh Valley	1-800-220-2733
Scranton, CCCS of Northeastern PA	**1-800-922-9537**
Sharon, CCCS of Warren	(412) 342-6302
State College, CCCS of Northeastern PA	1-800-922-9537
Stroudsburg, CCCS of Northeastern PA	1-800-922-9537
Sunbury, CCCS of Northeastern PA	1-800-922-9537
Tamaqua, CCCS of Lehigh Valley	1-800-220-2733

Trevose, CCCS/Delaware Valley	(215) 563-5665
Uniontown, CCCS of Western PA	(412) 439-8939
Washington, CCCS of Western PA	(412) 222-8292
West Chester, CCCS/Delaware Valley	(215) 563-5665
Whitehall, CCCS of Lehigh Valley	**(610) 821-4010**
Wilkes-Barre, CCCS of Northeastern PA	1-800-922-9537
Williamsport, CCCS of Northeastern PA	1-800-922-9537
York, CCCS of York	(717) 846-4176

RHODE ISLAND

East Providence, CCCS of Rhode Island	(401) 438-8833
Lincoln, CCCS of Rhode Island	(401) 732-1800
Newport, CCCS of Rhode Island	(401) 849-2227
Newport NETC, CCCS of Rhode Island	(401) 849-2227
Pawtucket, CCCS of Rhode Island	(401) 732-1800
Providence, CCCS of Rhode Island	(401) 274-7800
Wakefield, CCCS of Rhode Island	(401) 782-2070
Warwick, CCCS of Rhode Island	**(401) 732-1800**

SOUTH CAROLINA

Aiken, CCCS/Central Savannah River Area	1-800-736-0033
Anderson, CCCS/Compass of Carolina	(864) 467-3434
Barnwell, CCCS/Central Savannah River Area	1-800-736-0033
Charleston, Family Services CCC	**1-800-232-6489**
Columbia, CCCS Family Service Center	**1-800-223-9213**
Florence, CCCS Family Service Center	1-800-223-9213
Fort Jackson, CCCS Family Service Center	(803) 751-5256
Georgetown, Family Services CCC	1-800-232-6489
Greenville, CCCS/Compass of Carolina	**(864) 467-3434**
Greenwood, CCCS/Compass of Carolina	(864) 223-8694
Moncks Corner, Family Services CCC	1-800-232-6489
Rock Hill, CCCS Family Service Center	1-800-223-9213
Spartanburg, CCCS/Compass of Carolina	(864) 467-3434
Sumerville, Family Services CCC	1-800-232-6489
Sumter, CCCS Family Service Center	1-800-223-9213

SOUTH DAKOTA

Aberdeen, CCCS/Lutheran Social Services	1-888-258-2227
Brookings, CCCS/Lutheran Social Services	1-888-258-2227
Ellsworth AFB, CCCS of the Black Hills	(605) 348-4550
Huron, CCCS/Lutheran Social Services	1-888-258-2227
Mitchell, CCCS/Lutheran Social Services	1-888-258-2227
Mobridge, CCCS of the Black Hills	1-800-568-6615
Pierre, CCCS of the Black Hills	1-800-568-6615
Rapid City, CCCS of the Black Hills	**(605) 348-4550**
Sioux Falls, CCCS/Lutheran Social Services	1-888-258-2227
Sioux Falls, CCCS/Lutheran Social Services	**1-888-258-2227**
Spearfish, CCCS of the Black Hills	1-800-568-6615
Watertown, CCCS/Lutheran Social Services	1-888-258-2227
Yankton, CCCS/Lutheran Social Services	1-888-258-2227

TENNESSEE

Bartlett, Family Service of Memphis-CCCS	(901) 323-4909
Chattanooga, Family & Children's Services-CCCS	**(423) 490-5620**
Clarksville, CCCS of St. Louis	1-800-966-3328
Cleveland, Family & Children's Services-CCCS	(423) 490-5620
Columbia, CCCS of Middle TN	1-800-828-2227
Cookeville, CCCS of Middle TN	(615) 520-0043
Dayton, Family & Children's Services-CCCS	(423) 490-5620
Dickson, CCCS of Middle TN	(615) 227-3350
Dyersburg, Family Service of Memphis-CCCS	1-800-710-8902
Greeneville, CCCS of East Tennessee	(423) 928-2144
Hendersonville, CCCS of Middle TN	(615) 227-3350
Jackson, Family Service of Memphis-CCCS	1-800-710-8902
Johnson City, American Credit Counselors	1-800-646-0042
Johnson City, CCCS of East Tennessee	1-800-358-9231
Kingsport, CCCS of Southwestern Virginia	1-800-926-0042
Knoxville, CCCS of East Tennessee	**1-800-358-9231**
Leabanon, CCCS of Middle TN	(615) 227-3350
Maryville, CCCS of East Tennessee	(615) 522-2661
Memphis, Family Service of Memphis-CCCS	**(901) 323-4909**

Memphis, Family Service of Memphis-CCCS	(901) 323-4909
Morristown, CCCS of East Tennessee	1-800-358-9231
Murfreesboro, CCCS of Middle TN	(615) 890-2616
Nashville, CCCS of Middle TN	**(615) 227-3350**
Newport, CCCS of East Tennessee	1-800-358-9231
Oak Ridge, CCCS of East Tennessee	(423) 522-2661

TEXAS

Abilene, CCCS/Greater Fort Worth	1-800-374-2227
Alice, CCCS of South Texas	1-800-333-4357
Allen, CCCS of North Central Texas	1-800-856-0257
Amarillo, CCCS/Greater Dallas	(806) 358-2221
Aransas Pass, CCCS of South Texas	1-800-333-4357
Arlington, CCCS/Greater Dallas	(817) 461-2227
Athens, CCCS/Greater Dallas	1-800-396-2227
Austin, CCCS of Austin	**(512) 447-0711**
Azle, CCCS/Greater Fort Worth	(817) 732-2227
Bay City, CCCS/Gulf Coast Area	1-800-873-2227
Beaumont, CCCS/Gulf Coast Area	1-800-873-2227
Beeville, CCCS of South Texas	1-800-333-4357
Big Spring, CCCS/Greater Fort Worth	1-800-374-2227
Brady, CCCS/Greater Fort Worth	1-800-374-2227
Brenham, CCCS/Gulf Coast Area	1-800-873-2227
Brookhollow, CCCS/Gulf Coast Area	1-800-873-2227
Brownsville, CCCS of South Texas	1-800-333-4357
Brownwood, CCCS/Greater Fort Worth	1-800-646-2227
Bryan, CCCS/Gulf Coast Area	1-800-873-2227
Burleson, CCCS/Greater Fort Worth	1-800-374-2227
Carrollton, CCCS/Greater Dallas	(972) 242-6548
Cedar Hill, CCCS/Greater Dallas	(972) 291-4754
Cleburne, CCCS/Greater Fort Worth	(817) 641-4172
Corpus Christi, CCCS of South Texas	**1-800-333-4357**
Corsicana, CCCS/Greater Dallas	(903) 874-2227
Dalhart, CCCS/Greater Dallas	1-800-878-2227
Dallas/Parkway Plaza, CCCS/Greater Dallas	(972) 387-2227
Dallas/S Zang, CCCS/Greater Dallas	(214) 943-2075

Dallas, CCCS/Greater Dallas	(214) 363-4357
Dallas, CCCS/Greater Dallas	**(214) 638-2227**
Dallas/Pleasant Grove, Dallas, CCCS/Greater Dallas	(214) 388-7190
DeSoto, Dallas, CCCS/Greater Dallas	(972) 224-4786
Decatur, CCCS of North Central Texas	1-800-856-0257
Del Rio, CCCS/Greater San Antonio	1-800-410-2227
Denton, CCCS of North Central Texas	1-800-856-0257
Duncanville, CCCS/Greater Dallas	(972) 709-1723
East Harris County, CCCS/Gulf Coast Area	(713) 923-2227
El Paso, CCCS of the YWCA	**(915) 533-7475**
El Paso (East), CCCS of the YWCA	(915) 533-7475
El Paso (West), CCCS of the YWCA	(915) 533-7475
Ennis, CCCS/Greater Dallas	1-800-886-2227
Fort Hood, CCCS/Greater Fort Worth	1-800-374-2227
Fort Stockton, CCCS/Greater Fort Worth	(817) 732-2227
Fort Worth, CCCS/Greater Fort Worth	**1-800-374-2227**
Fort Worth/Downtown, CCCS/Greater Fort Worth	(817) 732-2227
Fort Worth/E, CCCS/Greater Fort Worth	(817) 561-0209
Fort Worth/N, CCCS/Greater Fort Worth	(817) 732-2227
Fort Worth/SW, CCCS/Greater Fort Worth	(817) 732-2227
Fort Worth/W, CCCS/Greater Fort Worth	(817) 732-2227
Fredericksburg, CCCS/Greater San Antonio	1-800-410-2227
Frisco, CCCS/North Central Texas	1-800-856-0257
Gainesville, CCCS/North Central Texas	1-800-856-0257
Galveston, CCCS/Gulf Coast Area	1-800-873-2227
Garland, CCCS/Greater Dallas	(972) 487-6461
Gatesville, CCCS/Greater Fort Worth	1-800-374-2227
Goodfellows AFB, CCCS/Greater Fort Worth	(915) 942-9156
Granbury, CCCS/Greater Fort Worth	1-800-374-2227
Grand Prairie, CCCS of Grand Prairie	(972) 642-3100
Grapevine, CCCS/Greater Fort Worth	(817) 732-2227
Greenville, CCCS/North Central Texas	1-800-856-0257
Gulfton, CCCS/Gulf Coast Area	(713) 923-2227
Harlingen, CCCS of South Texas	1-800-333-4357
Hereford, CCCS/Greater Dallas	1-800-878-2227
Hillsboro, CCCS/Greater Fort Worth	1-800-374-2227
Houston, CCCS/Gulf Coast Area	**(713) 923-2227**

Houston/Fannin, CCCS/Gulf Coast Area	(713) 923-2227
Houston/Fuqua, CCCS/Gulf Coast Area	(713) 923-2227
Houston/NW, CCCS/Gulf Coast Area	(713) 923-2227
Houston/Power Center, CCCS/Gulf Coast Area	(713) 923-2227
Houston/West, CCCS/Gulf Coast Area	(713) 923-2227
Humble, CCCS/Gulf Coast Area	(713) 923-2227
Huntsville, CCCS/Gulf Coast Area	1-800-873-2227
Hurst Mid-Cities, CCCS/Greater Fort Worth	(817) 732-2227
Irving, CCCS/Greater Dallas	(972) 255-0079
Jacksonville, CCCS/Greater Dallas	1-800-396-2227
Kerrville, CCCS/Greater San Antonio	1-800-410-2227
Kilgore, CCCS/Greater Fort Worth	1-800-374-2227
Kileen/Downtown, CCCS/Greater Fort Worth	1-800-374-2227
Kingsville, CCCS of South Texas	1-800-333-4357
Lake Jackson, CCCS/Gulf Coast Area	1-800-873-2227
Lampasas, CCCS/Greater Fort Worth	1-800-374-2227
Laredo, CCCS/Greater San Antonio	1-800-410-2227
Levelland, CCCS/Greater Fort Worth	1-800-374-2227
Lewisville, CCCS/North Central Texas	1-800-856-0257
Longview, CCCS/Greater Dallas	(903) 297-2900
Lubbock, CCCS/Greater Fort Worth	1-800-374-2227
Lufkin, CCCS/Gulf Coast Area	1-800-873-2227
Mansfield, CCCS/Greater Fort Worth	(817) 732-2227
Marshall, CCCS/Greater Dallas	1-800-577-2227
Mathis, CCCS of South Texas	1-800-333-4357
McAllen, CCCS of South Texas	1-800-333-4357
McKinney, CCCS/North Central Texas	**1-800-856-0257**
Mesquite, CCCS/Greater Dallas	(972) 681-2227
Mexia, CCCS/Greater Fort Worth	1-800-374-2227
Midland, CCCS/Greater Fort Worth	(915) 561-5540
Mineral Wells, CCCS/Greater Fort Worth	1-800-374-2227
Mt. Pleasant, CCCS/North Central Texas	1-800-856-0257
New Braunfels, CCCS/Greater San Antonio	1-800-410-2227
Odessa, CCCS/Greater Fort Worth	(915) 367-1180
Orange, CCCS/Gulf Coast Area	1-800-873-2227
Palestine, CCCS/Greater Dallas	1-800-396-2227
Pampa, CCCS/Greater Dallas	1-800-878-2227

Paris, CCCS/North Central Texas	1-800-856-0257
Plainview, CCCS/Greater Fort Worth	1-800-374-2227
Plano, CCCS/North Central Texas	1-800-856-0257
Port Arthur, CCCS/Gulf Coast Area	1-800-873-2227
Prarie View, CCCS/Gulf Coast Area	1-800-873-2227
Richardson, CCCS/Greater Dallas	(972) 437-6252
Robstown, CCCS of South Texas	1-800-333-4357
Rockwall, CCCS/Greater Dallas	(972) 722-1819
Round Rock, CCCS of Austin	(512) 447-0711
San Angelo, CCCS/Greater Fort Worth	1-800-374-2227
San Antonio/NE, CCCS/Greater San Antonio	(210) 979-4300
San Antonio, CCCS/Greater San Antonio	**(210) 979-4300**
San Antonio/S, CCCS/Greater San Antonio	(210) 979-4300
San Marcos, CCCS of Austin	(512) 396-4599
Seguin, CCCS/Greater San Antonio	1-800-410-2227
Sherman, CCCS/North Central Texas	1-800-856-0257
Sonora, CCCS/Greater Fort Worth	1-800-374-2227
South Post Oak, CCCS/Gulf Coast Area	(713) 923-2227
Spring, CCCS/Gulf Coast Area	(713) 923-2227
Stafford, CCCS/Gulf Coast Area	(713) 923-2227
Stephenville, CCCS/Greater Fort Worth	(817) 965-7441
Sulphur Springs, CCCS/North Central Texas	1-800-856-0257
Sunnyside, CCCS/Gulf Coast Area	(713) 923-2227
Sweetwater, CCCS/Greater Fort Worth	1-800-374-2227
Temple, CCCS/Greater Fort Worth	1-800-374-2227
Terrell, CCCS/Greater Dallas	(972) 551-2227
Texarkana, CCCS/North Central Texas	1-800-856-0257
Texas City, CCCS/Gulf Coast Area	1-800-873-2227
The Colony, CCCS/North Central Texas	1-800-856-0257
Tyler, CCCS/Greater Dallas	(903) 581-6691
Uvalde, CCCS/Greater San Antonio	1-800-410-2227
Vernon, CCCS/Greater Dallas	1-800-380-2227
Victoria, CCCS of South Texas	1-800-333-4357
Waco, CCCS/Greater Fort Worth	(254) 772-0007
Waxahachie, CCCS/Greater Dallas	(972) 938-9672
Weatherford, CCCS/Greater Fort Worth	1-800-374-2227
Wichita Falls, CCCS/Greater Dallas	(817) 696-2227

UTAH

Ogden, CCCS of Utah	(801) 394-7759
West Jordan, CCCS of Utah	**(801) 566-0800**

VERMONT

Barre, CCCS of NH & VT	1-800-327-6778
Bennington, CCCS of NH & VT	1-800-327-6778
Brattleboro, CCCS of NH & VT	1-800-327-6778
Burlington, CCCS of NH & VT	1-800-327-6778
Rutland, CCCS of NH & VT	1-800-327-6778

VIRGINIA

Alexandria, CCCS/Greater Washington	1-800-747-4222
Arlington, CCCS/Greater Washington	1-800-747-4222
Bristol, CCCS of Southwestern Virginia	1-800-926-0042
Cedar Bluff, CCCS of Bluefield	1-800-313-5097
Charlottesville, CCCS of Virginia	(804) 977-9596
Chesapeake, CCCS of Virginia	(757) 548-9406
Christiansburg, CCCS of Southwestern VA	1-800-926-0042
Colonial Heights, CCCS of Virginia	(804) 520-8744
Covington, CCCS of Southwestern VA	1-800-926-0042
Culpeper, CCCS of Virginia	(703) 825-5394
Danville, CCCS of Virginia	(804) 792-2227
Fairfax, CCCS/Greater Washington	1-800-747-4222
Farmville, CCCS of Virginia	(804) 392-7646
Fort Eustis, CCCS of Hampton Roads	1-800-311-2927
Fredericksburg, CCCS of Virginia	(703) 371-7575
Hampton, Credit Counselors-Tidewater	(757) 825-2227
Hampton, CCCS of Hampton Roads	**(757) 826-2227**
Harrisonburg, CCCS of Virginia	(540) 564-1471
Langley AFB, CCCS of Hampton Roads	1-800-311-2927
Leesburg, CCCS/Greater Washington	1-800-747-4222
Lynchburg, American Credit Counselors	1-800-646-0042

Lynchburg, CCCS of Central Virginia	**(804) 847-4447**
Manassas, CCCS/Greater Washington	1-800-747-4222
Martinsville, CCCS of Southwestern VA	1-800-926-0042
Mechanicsville, CCCS of Virginia	(804) 746-5180
Midlothian, CCCS of Virginia	(804) 379-4505
Newport News, CCCS of Hampton Roads	(757) 826-2227
Newport News, CCCS of Hampton Roads	1-800-311-2827
Newport News, Credit Counselors-Tidewater	(757) 874-2900
Norfolk, Credit Counselors-Tidewater	(757) 531-2227
Portsmouth, CCCS of Portsmouth	**(757) 397-2121**
Portsmouth, CCCS of Virginia	(757) 488-2227
Richmond, CCCS of Virginia	**(804) 780-9042**
Richmond (East), CCCS of Virginia	(804) 222-1134
Richmond (West), CCCS of Virginia	(804) 270-0976
Roanoke, CCCS of Southwestern VA	**(540) 366-2227**
Staunton, CCCS of Virginia	(540) 885-4799
Virginia Beach, Catholic Charities/Hampton Roads	**(757) 467-7707**
Virginia Beach #1, CCCS of Virginia	(757) 424-2060
Virginia Beach #2, CCCS of Virginia	(757) 473-2227
Virginia Beach #3, CCCS of Virginia	(757) 425-3328
Williamsburg, CCCS of Hampton Roads	(757) 826-2227
Winchester, CCCS/Greater Washington	1-800-747-4222
Woodbridge, CCCS/Greater Washington	1-800-747-4222

WASHINGTON

Aberdeen, CCCS/Olympic-South Sound	1-800-244-1183
Bellevue, CCCS of Seattle	1-800-634-2227
Bellingham, CCCS of Seattle	1-800-634-2227
Bremerton, CCCS/Olympic-South Sound	1-800-244-1183
Chehalis, CCCS/Olympic-South Sound	1-800-244-1183
Colville, CCCS/Inland Northwest	1-800-892-6854
Everett, CCCS of Seattle	1-800-634-2227
Fort Lewis, CCCS/Olympic-South Sound	1-800-244-1183
Kennewick, CCCS of the Tri-Cities	**(509) 586-2181**
Kent, CCCS of Seattle	1-800-634-2227

Longview, CCCS of Oregon	(360) 425-4520
McChord AFB, CCCS/Olympic-South Sound	(206) 588-1858
Moses Lake, CCCS of Yakima Valley	1-800-273-6897
Mountlake Terrace, CCCS of Seattle	1-800-634-2227
Mt. Vernon, CCCS of Seattle	1-800-634-2227
Oak Harbor, CCCS of Seattle	1-800-634-2227
Olympia, CCCS/Olympic-South Sound	1-800-244-1183
Port Angeles, Community Credit Counselors	(360) 417-2692
Port Angeles, CCCS/Olympic-South Sound	1-800-244-1183
Poulsbo, CCCS/Olympic-South Sound	1-800-244-1183
Puyallup, CCCS/Olympic-South Sound	(206) 588-1858
Raymond, CCCS/Olympic-South Sound	1-800-244-1183
Seattle, CCCS of Seattle	**1-800-634-2227**
Seattle/Downtown, CCCS of Seattle	1-800-634-2227
Shelton, CCCS/Olympic-South Sound	1-800-244-1183
Silverdale, CCCS of Seattle	(360) 698-1220
South Bend, CCCS/Olympic-South Sound	1-800-244-1183
Spokane, CCCS/Inland Northwest	**(509) 327-3777**
Sunnyside, CCCS of Yakima Valley	1-800-273-6897
Tacoma, Community Credit Counselors	(206) 475-6387
Tacoma, CCCS/Olympic-South Sound	**(206) 588-1858**
Tumwater, CCCS/Olympic-South Sound	1-800-244-1183
U.S. Sub Base Banger, CCCS/Olympic-South Sound	1-800-244-1183
Vancouver, CCCS of Oregon	(360) 694-7564
Walla Walla, CCCS of the Tri-Cities	(509) 525-2132
Wenatchee, CCCS of Yakima Valley	(509) 662-0936
Yakima, CCCS of Yakima Valley	**(509) 248-5270**

WEST VIRGINIA

Beckley, CCCS of Southern WV	**(304) 255-2499**
Bluefield, CCCS of Bluefield	**(304) 325-5143**
Buckhannon, CCCS of North Central WV	1-800-498-6681
Charleston, CCCS of the Kanawha Valley	**1-800-281-5969**
Chester, CCCS of the Upper Ohio Valley	1-800-220-3252
Clarksburg, CCCS of North Central WV	**(304) 623-0921**
Elizabeth, CCCS of the Mid-Ohio Valley	1-800-882-4924

Elkins, CCCS of North Central WV	1-800-498-6682
Fairmont, CCCS of North Central WV	(304) 366-3331
Harrisville, CCCS of the Mid-Ohio Valley	1-800-882-4924
Huntington, CCCS of Family Service	**(304) 522-4321**
Logan, CCCS of the Kanawha Valley	1-800-281-5969
Martinsburg, CCCS/Greater Washington	1-800-747-4222
Morgantown, CCCS of North Central WV	(304) 291-6819
New Martinsville, CCCS/Upper Ohio Valley	1-800-220-3252
Parkersburg, CCCS/Mid-Ohio Valley	**1-800-882-4924**
Philippi, CCCS of North Central WV	1-800-498-6681
Pt. Pleasant, CCCS/Mid-Ohio Valley	1-800-882-4924
Ravenswood, CCCS/Mid-Ohio Valley	1-800-882-4924
Sistersville, CCCS/Mid-Ohio Valley	1-800-882-4924
Spencer, CCCS/Mid-Ohio Valley	1-800-882-4924
St. Marys, CCCS/Mid-Ohio Valley	1-800-882-4924
Wheeling, CCCS/Upper Ohio Valley	**(304) 232-7237**

WISCONSIN

Beloit, CCCS of Madison	(608) 365-1244
Eau Claire, CCCS/Family Service St. Croix	1-800-780-2890
Fond du Lac, CCCS of Sheboygan	1-800-350-2227
Green Bay, CCCS of Northeastern WI	(414) 437-7531
La Crosse, CCCS of La Crosse	**(608) 782-0704**
Madison, CCCS of Madison	**(608) 252-1320**
Manitowoc, CCCS of Northeastern WI	(414) 684-6651
Menasha, CCCS of Northeastern WI	**(414) 727-8300**
Milwaukee, CCCS of Milwaukee	(414) 456-1480
Milwaukee, CCCS of Milwaukee	(414) 456-1480
Milwaukee, CCCS of Milwaukee	**(414) 456-1480**
Milwaukee/Bayshore, CCCS of Milwaukee	(414) 456-1480
Racine, CCCS of Racine	**(414) 634-2391**
Sheboygan, CCCS of Sheboygan	**(414) 458-3784**
Sturgeon Bay, CCCS of Northeastern WI	(414) 734-1862
Waukesha, CCCS of Milwaukee	(414) 456-1480
Wausau, CCCS of LaCrosse	(715) 849-3322

WYOMING

Casper, CCCS of Greater Wyoming	(307) 234-8771
Cheyenne, CCCS of N CO & SE WY	1-800-424-2227
Gillette, CCCS of Greater Wyoming	**(307) 687-7747**
Laramie, CCCS of N CO & SE WY	1-800-424-2227

PUERTO RICO

Aguadilla, CCCS of Puerto Rico	(787) 722-8835
Bayamon, CCCS of Puerto Rico	(787) 722-8835
Carolina, CCCS of Puerto Rico	(787) 722-8835
Ponce, CCCS of Puerto Rico	(787) 722-8835
Santurce, CCCS of Puerto Rico	**(787) 722-8835**

CANADA

Grimsby, Ontario Association	**(905) 945-5644**
New Brunswick, CCCS of Maine	1-800-539-2227
Toronto, CCCS of Metropolitan Toronto	**(416) 593-7434**

Boldface offices are administrative locations.

Index

AFTERWORD

WITH RESOLVE, WE CHANGE bad habits to good habits. We learn from our mistakes, and hopefully, through the use of this book, you can put what you have learned into action. I hope it introduces you to a rich and fulfilling life.

The next step is up to you. I hope you will take it. As you navigate through the waters to financial freedom, tell me your experiences. Let me know where this book can be improved, and most of all, how it has help you!

Warmest regards,

Carolyn J. White
Author, *Debt No More*

Attention:

Corporations, Professional Organizations, Colleges, Universities, Associations, and Special Groups

Quantity discounts are available for bulk purchases of this book for educational training purposes, fund raising, gifts, etc.

The author is available for seminars and lectures. For more information, contact:

Clifton House Publishing, LLC
P. O. Box 5034
Springfield, Va. 22150

Toll Free: 1-(888) A WAY FREE (292-9373)

ORDER FORM

Fax Orders:	(703) 222-6044
Telephone Orders:	Call Toll Free
	1 (888) A WAY FREE
	(292-9373)
	Have your VISA or MasterCard ready:
Postal Orders:	Clifton House Publishing, LLC
	P.O. Box 5034-B
	Springfield, Va. 22150

Please send the following books:

Book	Quantity	Unit Price		Total
Debt No More	_____ x	$ 14.95	=	_____
Money Harmony	_____ x	$ 9.95	=	_____
Overcoming Overspending	_____ x	$ 12.95	=	_____

Virginia Residents Add 4.5% Sales Tax _____

Add Shipping & Handling $4.95 for the first
book & $2.00 for each additional book. _____

Total _____

Ship To:

Name: _____

Company Name: _____

Address: _____

_____

Zip Code_____

Payment: Check or Money Order _____

Credit Card: _____ Visa _____ MasterCard

Card Number: _____

Expiration Date: _____

Name On Card: _____

Call Toll Free and Order Now

ORDER FORM

Fax Orders:	(703) 222-6044
Telephone Orders:	Call Toll Free
	1 (888) A WAY FREE
	(292-9373)
	Have your VISA or MasterCard ready:
Postal Orders:	Clifton House Publishing, LLC
	P.O. Box 5034-B
	Springfield, Va. 22150

Please send the following books:

Book	Quantity	Unit Price		Total
Debt No More	_____ x	$ 14.95	=	_____
Money Harmony	_____ x	$ 9.95	=	_____
Overcoming Overspending	_____ x	$ 12.95	=	_____

Virginia Residents Add 4.5% Sales Tax   _____

Add Shipping & Handling $4.95 for the first
book & $2.00 for each additional book.   _____

Total   _____

Ship To:

Name: _____

Company Name: _____

Address: _____

_____

Zip Code_____

Payment: Check or Money Order _____

Credit Card: _____Visa _____MasterCard

Card Number: _____

Expiration Date: _____

Name On Card: _____

Call Toll Free and Order Now

ORDER FORM

Fax Orders: (703) 222-6044

Telephone Orders: Call Toll Free
                                 1 (888) A WAY FREE
                                     (292-9373)
                                 Have your VISA or MasterCard ready:

Postal Orders: Clifton House Publishing, LLC
                                   P.O. Box 5034-B
                                   Springfield, Va. 22150

Please send the following books:

Book	Quantity	Unit Price		Total
Debt No More	_____ x	$ 14.95	=	_____
Money Harmony	_____ x	$ 9.95	=	_____
Overcoming Overspending	_____ x	$ 12.95	=	_____

               Virginia Residents Add 4.5% Sales Tax   _____

               Add Shipping & Handling $4.95 for the first
               book & $2.00 for each additional book.   _____

                                        Total   _____

Ship To:

    Name: _____

    Company Name: _____

    Address: _____

                      _____

                             Zip Code_____

Payment: Check or Money Order   _____

Credit Card: _____Visa _____MasterCard

Card Number: _____

Expiration Date: _____

Name On Card: _____

Call Toll Free and Order Now

ORDER FORM

Fax Orders:	(703) 222-6044
Telephone Orders:	Call Toll Free
	1 (888) A WAY FREE
	(292-9373)
	Have your VISA or MasterCard ready:
Postal Orders:	Clifton House Publishing, LLC
	P.O. Box 5034-B
	Springfield, Va. 22150

Please send the following books:

Book	Quantity	Unit Price	Total
Debt No More	_____ x	$ 14.95 =	_____
Money Harmony	_____ x	$ 9.95 =	_____
Overcoming Overspending	_____ x	$ 12.95 =	_____

Virginia Residents Add 4.5% Sales Tax _____

Add Shipping & Handling $4.95 for the first
book & $2.00 for each additional book. _____

Total _____

Ship To:

Name: _____

Company Name: _____

Address: _____

_____

Zip Code_____

Payment: Check or Money Order _____

Credit Card: _____Visa _____MasterCard

Card Number: _____

Expiration Date: _____

Name On Card: _____

Call Toll Free and Order Now